AFTER THE TEARS

Parents Talk about
Raising a Child with a Disability

ROBIN SIMONS

HARCOURT BRACE JOVANOVICH, PUBLISHERS

San Diego   New York   London

The names of some of the parents quoted have been changed at their request. Some of the quotations have been combined for the sake of fluent narrative.

Library of Congress Cataloging-in-Publication Data
Simons, Robin.
   After the tears.
   Reprint. Originally published: Denver, Colo. :
Children's Museum of Denver, c1985.
   "A Harvest/HBJ book."
   Bibliography: p.
   1. Parents of handicapped children—United States—Attitudes. 2. Handicapped children—United States—Family relationships. I. Title.
[HQ759.913.S56   1987]   649'.151   86-31884
ISBN 0-15-103963-1
ISBN 0-15-602900-6 (pbk.)

Printed in the United States of America
First edition
A B C D E

In parenting a child with a disability you face a major choice. You can believe that your child's condition is a death blow to everything you've dreamed and worked toward until now. Or you can decide that you will continue to lead the life you'd planned—and incorporate your child into it. Parents who choose the latter course find they do a tremendous amount of growing. They find inner strengths they didn't know they had. They develop a greater sense of self-esteem. They develop an openness about their feelings and an ability to share those feelings with each other. *After the Tears* is the story of many such parents— parents who have struggled, learned and grown in the years since their children were born. All of them felt the same initial anguish on learning of their child's disability. All have come a long way since those initial tears. They share their stories with you to give you the benefit of their experiences, to let you know you're not alone, and to offer you encouragement in growing with and loving your child.

Lib Cummings

One Family's Story

Allen Birnbach

Mark and Barbara Buswell lived in the mountains outside of Colorado Springs. They and their year-old son, Brook, enjoyed their rural life and had just bought ten acres of land on which to build a solar home. June 1 was the date for breaking ground. On May 6, Mark rushed Barb to the hospital where she gave birth to Wilson. Wilson was born with cerebral palsy.

In the early days of Wilson's life he needed specialized neonatal care and was rushed to a different hospital from the one Barb was in. While she recovered, Mark shuttled between work, home and the two hospitals, caring for Brook, listening to doctors' reports on Wilson's condition and bringing Barb pictures of the new baby. After several weeks of this frenzied existence, Barb and Wilson came home. The initial shock had worn off, and Barb and Mark had a chance to think. The reality of their son's handicap hit them like the proverbial ton of bricks.

Immediately Barb became busy. She read everything she could get her hands on about cerebral palsy. She became wholly absorbed in Wilson and organized her life around meeting his needs. His needs were constant. He had to be fed every hour and a half, but each feeding took an hour because he had difficulty swallowing. He needed therapy three times a week in town, but driving down the mountain roads, he threw up all the food she had worked so hard to give him. Caring for him in other ways left very little time for Barb to spend with Brook, who had one-and-a-half-year-old needs of his own.

Mark reacted differently. He withdrew. He didn't read books, he didn't play with Wilson or do much therapy with him. In fact he didn't attach himself to Wilson much at all. He wasn't at all sure he wanted this baby who had thrown his life into chaos, stolen his wife away, and made them both unhappy. Mark was angry —very angry—that things were so wretched in his family now. "Where's my normal baby?" he demanded, "my normal family? What about those things we used to do—go camping, spend time with each other, have fun?!

> "Where's my normal baby? My normal family?"

All our normal life is out the window!"

As Mark got angrier and more withdrawn, Barb got angry, too. She was angry that this situation had caused such frightening disruption, but she was even angrier at Mark for being so withdrawn. It was hard for her to see him not attach himself to their son, and she felt abandoned to the problems of raising him. Mark had had a share in causing those problems and now he wasn't even helping solve them! She redoubled her efforts over the two boys as she and Mark grew farther apart.

Mark began spending less time at home. He stayed later at work and found lots of little errands to do on the way home. "I got more dry cleaning done that year than in the rest of my life," he said, "because I didn't want to come home and face this family that was falling apart."

"I got more dry cleaning done that year than in the rest of my life..."

At the end of the first year, both parents felt, "How much longer can our family take this?" Needless to say they hadn't broken ground on the new house.

Then two things happened. Instead of starting the house, they decided to move to town. That would make life easier, they thought. They would be closer to the doctor and to therapy. Mark's "errand time" would be shorter and he could spend more time at home. Plus they would be near neighbors and wouldn't feel so isolated with their problems.

The second thing was that Barb decided to visit her brother who lived in another state. They had always been close; she could talk to him. He was removed from their problems and could be more objective.

These two decisions marked a turning point for the family. Barb returned from her brother's revitalized. He had helped her see herself as capable and powerful, the two qualities she'd felt most lacking. The move to town produced all the positive benefits they had imagined. Shortly after they moved in, they found that another family with a handicapped child lived close by, and for the first time they had people with whom they could share their concerns. They attended a conference for parents of children with disabilities and discovered that the prison of strain in which they had felt confined since Wilson's birth was common to every couple there. They found they could even offer some advice and solace to other couples. With this new perspective, Barb and Mark could see a light at the end of the tunnel.

Another pivotal event occurred about this time. They decided to buy Wilson a wheelchair. Buying a wheelchair was a hard decision. It meant admitting to themselves and to the world that their son was handicapped. Wilson in a stroller was just another baby. Wilson in a pint-size wheelchair was a statement. But they did it, and they found that people in supermarkets still came up to them and said, "Oh what a cute little boy." Some also asked about his problem. Some just stared. So Mark and Barb learned how to talk to strangers about cerebral palsy and how to be proud and private even in public. They moved on to new adjustments to Wilson's disability. But they had gotten through the hardest time.

A SUGGESTION

Scrapbook of Success
Make a scrapbook for your child. Put in:
- *photos*
- *drawings*
- *things he's made*
- *his favorite pictures*
- *a piece of his security blanket…*

Record:
- *his growth*
- *his changes*
- *his first word*
- *his favorite things…*

Connie Lehman

**"W**hat's supposed to be the best day of your life turns out to be like a funeral."

For some parents it begins the day their child is born. For others there are weeks, months, even years of foreboding—knowing but not knowing that something is wrong. At some point it is confirmed by a doctor: your child is not the perfect baby you expected. Then the struggle to cope begins.

As soon as a woman becomes pregnant, both parents begin to fantasize about the child they will have. The child will be perfect—beautiful, successful, all the things the parents would like to be themselves. Sometimes they talk about these dreams together. Sometimes they don't even realize they have them...until their child is born. Then suddenly they hit. In the case of a child with a disability, parents spend much of the child's early life learning to accept that the child they have is not the child they wanted.

The initial reaction is usually shock and panic. "I can't handle this! What will I do?!" They are terrified—afraid that they will not be able to cope with the situation; afraid of the future—both theirs and their child's—which they assume will be terrible. One mother of a six-month-old said, "It was so good to see another family with a child with Down syndrome, to see that he's not a monster." Deep down, that's what she feared for her own son.

This kind of terror is hard to bear so most parents quickly begin searching for answers—for information that will enable them to understand and cope with the news. What they hope to find out is that it was a mistake, that the child they wanted—the one they were really supposed to have—is still waiting to come out. They look for signs that this may be true. They look for doctors who will encourage that hope. "We went through a period of changing doctors. Dragging John around from one to the next so they could all evaluate him. There was something wrong with every one of them. One I didn't like because he was old and I figured he wasn't keeping up on the newest advances. Another one I didn't like because he said, 'Yes, it's spina bifida, he'll never walk or move his legs.' I thought, 'How do you know what he'll never do?' Finally we went to a doctor who said he didn't know what the extent of John's handicap would be, we'd have to wait and see, and we stayed with him. That was easier to take than the others. What I was really looking for was someone who would tell me what I wanted to hear—that it would go away."

They look for cures. "I hate it when they give you generalities. Give me specific exercises to do! I want to do everything I can for Peter. Maybe we can solve his problems."

And they bargain. "I wish they'd made *me* blind instead of her. I've already seen the world. But she's too small..."

This searching for an "out" is normal—even healthy. It gives you time to recover from the shock of discovering your child is handicapped, to gather your emotional strength and keep on going. It only becomes unhealthy if you get stuck there, refusing to accept your child's condition. He needs to be loved *with* his disability, not in spite of it. You need to integrate his handicap into your lives. Only that way can you help him develop to his fullest potential.

"I've heard this period called 'nothingness' and that's exactly how you feel. You can't move, can't think, can't do anything but feel—leaden, like a rock. There's nothing there—but that disability."

Little by little, parents accept the fact that the search is fruitless. All the hoping, all the doctors, all the special treatments won't make the handicap go away. Gradually they face the reality of the situation: their child is handicapped and it will have a profound effect on their lives. Now the tables seem to turn 180°. Whereas before they were intent on affirming the child's normalcy, now they see nothing but the disability. The child as an individual becomes secondary as the handicap becomes overwhelming, the focus of their lives. They begin a frantic search for the cause, casting blame on themselves and on each other. Each parent, regardless of the actual cause, feels guilty.

3

At the same time they feel angry—at the doctor who told them for being insensitive, for not preventing the handicap, for not making it go away; at each other for not solving the problem; at the unfairness of the situation, and at the child himself for having disappointed them so badly.

Coupled with the grief, guilt and anger is a sense of confusion: there are so many questions without answers, so much uncertainty about the future, so much frustration. And it's all compounded by the bone-breaking exhaustion of catering to the endless demands of a baby with a disability.

The assault is so great that most parents become paralyzed. Weighed down by their feelings, they become incapable of making decisions. They know that help is out there but they are unable to pick up the phone to ask for it. In the face of the senseless thing that has happened to them they feel powerless, victimized, isolated—alone in facing their problems, stranded from their former life, but unwilling, mistaken visitors in a new one.

Every family moves out of "nothingness" in its own way and at its own speed. Gradually parents begin to see the whole child—his smile, his perseverance, the things he can do well—instead of just the handicap. They begin to notice that he looks like someone in the family—and take pride in it! The gap between the child they wanted and the child they have gets smaller, until they find themselves *wanting* the child they have.

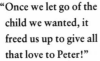

"Once we let go of the child we wanted, it freed us up to give all that love to Peter!"

Barbara Collins explains joyfully how it happened for them. "Once we let go of the child we wanted, it freed us up to give all that love to Peter!"

For most parents, the process begins with a choice. "We got tired of feeling victimized," says one father, "so we decided to do something that would help us feel more powerful. We joined a parents group at our daughter's preschool. By meeting other parents and finding out we weren't alone, we began to feel we *could* gain some control over our lives."

Other families make other decisions. Lee and Roberta Constantine decided that Roberta would go back to work, even though at first she didn't want to. But getting out into the world where their son's Down syndrome was not the only focus turned out to be exactly the motivating force they needed. It helped them realize that Greg's handicap could be woven into their lives without dominating them completely.

Cathy and Craig Packer decided to have another child. For a long time after their son, Christian, was born with Down syndrome, both felt strongly that he would be their only child—in part because of their desire to give him every possible benefit and in part because of their fear of giving birth to another handicapped child. When Christian was two, though, Cathy became pregnant, and from the moment she found out, she knew she would have the baby.

Suddenly she realized that there was room in her life and her heart to care for and love another child. For both parents the decision to have the second child marked a turning point—an awakening to a life in which Christian's handicap was just a part, not the whole thing.

> "My philosophy of life is that it's like being on a beach. You get knocked down by a wave and you can either lie there and drown, or you can get up and move. If you don't keep moving you die."

Whatever the decision, the impetus and the result for each family are the same: the regaining of power in their lives. Chuck Cloud describes how it worked for him. "My philosophy of life is that it's like being on a beach. You get knocked down by a wave and you can either lie there and drown, or you can get up and move. If you don't keep moving you die." After many months of "just lying there" his family was ready to move.

As parents start to feel more in control, external elements begin to fall into place. They find some professionals whom they trust. They find friends with whom they can talk and who take an interest in their child. Frequently they join parents groups to meet others with the same concerns. They begin to accept the handicap and to integrate it into their lives.

Karen Klish knew she had "made it" when she picked up the mail one day and found her son John's audiology report in it. John is profoundly deaf, but as she read through the report, Karen was able to say to herself, "That's a piece of paper. That's not John." She could separate John and his handicap.

Recovery is not final. "You don't just recover and go on," points out Dave Hightower, whose ten-year-old son, Kevin, has cerebral palsy. "It's an ongoing process. You have to continually monitor yourself and your family to keep a handle on how you're all doing, and make an effort to meet your own needs. It's a challenge to not burn out."

You also recycle through the grief process. Birthdays, holidays, missed milestones retrigger the sadness, guilt and anger. Those feelings never go away. "But each time it's less intense," says Paula Hightower, Dave's wife. "It's not as frightening or overwhelming, and it's quicker. You don't believe you ever will at the beginning, but you get stronger," she adds. "You make it."

A SUGGESTION

Don't think of your child as a "handicapped child." Think of him as a "child who has a handicap." He's a child first, like all other children. His handicap is secondary.

Write down all the things he's done in the last week that have made you laugh and smile.

This model of emotional stages that parents go through on learning of their child's disability was developed by Dr. Gilbert M. Foley, Director of the Family Centered Resource Center, 3010 St. Lawrence Avenue, Reading, Pennsylvania 19606.

Peter Hoey

"I f God punished people by giving them handicapped children, everyone would have one."

"Why?!" exclaims Anna Sitzman, mother of a child who is multiply handicapped. "I'm obsessed with why this happened to me!" Like most parents of children with disabilities, she faces the question of why—over and over again.

On one level you're looking for a physiological cause. On another level you're looking for something bigger—not for the reason it happened, but for the reason it happened to you. Why were you singled out? Where is the sense in this seemingly senseless situation?

Unfortunately, there's no absolute answer to that question. Since that's hard to accept, most parents create their own by taking the blame on themselves.

"I feel like God abandoned me. I believe in him. But I feel like I must have done something wrong and now he's punishing me."

"I should have quit my job earlier. I was under too much stress."

"I should have made her quit her job when she got pregnant."

"If only I hadn't smoked while I was pregnant..."

The fact of the matter, though, is that most handicaps are caused by factors beyond your control. Feeling guilty—while normal—is uncalled for. It's also counterproductive. Jo Lynn Lei is the Director of Membership and Family Support for the Association for Retarded Citizens of Jefferson County, Colorado. She advises, "You have to come to grips with there being no answer to why it happened to you. Then you can go on and live your life. The longer you hang on to feeling guilty, the harder you make it on yourself and the more frustrated you'll be in every situation. Guilt over causing the handicap becomes guilt that you can't make everything else perfect for your child. Feeling guilty doesn't do a thing to help your child. You might as well channel that energy into constructive action."

Some parents must face the fact that they *were* responsible for causing their child's handicap. If this has been confirmed by your doctor, you must learn to live with that knowledge. But again, don't dwell on it. Wallowing in guilt, self-reproach or self-pity does nothing to help your child. It only prevents you from doing everything you can to make the most of your lives. Accept the situation and move on.

A second level of guilt commonly plagues parents of children with disabilities. "We feel guilty that we're not doing everything we can for our child," says one couple. A father bemoans his guilt at being "less than the perfect parent and spouse." A mother who works days and caters to the needs of her multiply handicapped son at night feels guilty "at not meeting the needs of the rest of the family." This desire to be superparent and superspouse is understandable—but unrealistic. No parent can be a loving parent or perfect spouse all the time. No parent can meet all his child's needs. You are only human, no more. Pushing yourself to do more than you can do only makes you tired, resentful and angry. That is counterproductive for you, your family and your child.

Anger can be equally insidious. "We purposely started our family young so we could travel at 50," says Kathy Taylor whose second child was born with Down syndrome. "This interferes with our plan. I'm angry at her for that! I'm angry at her for making me go back to work. I'm angry at her for being handicapped! I know that's unreasonable, but I am."

> "I'm angry at her for being handicapped! I know that's unreasonable, but I am."

Anger at your child for being handicapped is very hard to admit. How can you feel angry at someone for something that's not his fault (especially when it's the child who has to live with the handicap)? But all parents feel angry at their handicapped children for the tremendous disruption they inject into their lives. That anger, in turn, breeds more guilt. "I love Dan. He's a wonderful child and I feel like I shouldn't say this. But sometimes I hate him for being handicapped and for making our life so hard. I see other kids and I wish Dan could be like that. And then I feel so *guilty* for thinking those things."

The financial demands of a child's disability are another source of resentment and anger. "It's expensive raising a child with a handicap. Dan's therapy isn't covered by insurance. I worry about that. I worry what would happen if I lost my job. I feel like I've lost some flexibility in my career and I get resentful when I think about that."

Most parents even wish occasionally that their child would die. As one mother admitted, "Sometimes I wish she'd die. And then I feel horrible and guilty for having that thought."

Anger and guilt toward your child are difficult feelings to cope with. But they are very natural...and very common. The important thing is to recognize them when they occur—not to pretend they aren't there. By burying anger you cause it to spread—to your spouse, to professionals, to the world. By burying guilt you make it a poison that eats away at your effectiveness and self-worth.

Talk about your feelings! Talking helps dissipate the feelings and enables you to work through them. Sharing them with your spouse will draw you closer together and solidify your marriage. ◆

A SUGGESTION

Make a list of the things you feel guilty about. Talk over the list with another person. Cross off the ones you're not responsible for. Cross off the ones you can't change. Make a plan of action for dealing with the rest.

Hunter Freeman

"Every day you overcome a barrier...then there's a new one..."

Jo Lynn Lei is the mother of a nine-year-old boy who has cerebral palsy. When David was four, doctors said he would never walk. Unwilling to accept that, Jo Lynn refused to buy a wheelchair and encouraged her son to crawl about on his own. When David was eight, his doctor suggested that surgery to loosen the tight muscles in his legs might enhance his mobility. It would be a serious operation, however, and its success would not be guaranteed. The family opted for the surgery. To their tremendous relief it was successful, and within months, David was able to stand up and walk slowly with a walker. His excitement was unbounded, and with characteristic determination, he was up and moving and working on his walking at every opportunity. The entire family was overjoyed. Several months later David's therapist announced that she had begun to see signs of scoliosis in David's spine. They were brought on, she felt, by his newly increased mobility. As Jo Lynn said, "You don't get very long to rejoice."

The problems seem relentless. From frequent colds to medical crises, from skirmishes with bus aides to battles with principals, life with a handicapped child is not easy. As one mother says, "All I wanted was a baby and now I've got doctors' appointments, therapy appointments, surgeries, medical bills, a strained marriage, no more free time... When you have a handicapped child, you don't just have to deal with the child and the fact that he's handicapped. You have to adjust to a whole new way of life. It's a double whammy." Another mother concurs, "Every day you overcome a barrier and then there's a new one. Just when you feel like you've had a success: BANG! there's a new problem."

Luckily, parents learn to handle the assaults. Whether out of practice or necessity, you become resilient, more able to meet the next challenge than you ever thought you would be. "My friends say, 'How can you handle all the problems you have?' I never thought of myself as a strong person, but I guess I've become one."

"Just when you feel like you've had a success: BANG! there's a new problem."

Another mother agrees. "The problems don't go away, they just change. But after a while you realize you can get through them."

Where does this resilience come from? It comes from loving your child. "John needs, so I do it," says one mother. "There's really no question. Sometimes I get real 'whacked out' from it, so tired of one thing after another. But I love him and that keeps me going."

Barbara Collins agrees. "You count the successes, not the disappointments. There are a lot of disappointments, for sure. But there are also a lot of joys. Peter's birthday party—just to see how happy all those kids were—that goes a long way toward helping me get through the tough times."

Jane Scott speaks for many parents when she says, "There are a lot of problems, and many of them are huge. You think, 'How can I get through this?' But if you put all the disappointments on a scale and put all the joys on the other side, the joys would weigh a lot more."

Learning to take one day at a time also helps. As Jane Scott says, "You learn to take things as they come, not to look ahead and worry about what the next crisis will be. You just take every day, one day at a time."

Some parents counterbalance the problems by celebrating the joys and triumphs. "Sure there are lots of problems. But you can't dwell on them. We celebrate every victory. Every time Christine learns a new skill or crosses a hurdle we throw a party. She probably doesn't realize what they're for, but it helps us!"

Many families find their greatest support comes from other, similar families. "I talk to other parents. It doesn't make the problems go away. But it helps you just to be able to talk. With everyone else you have to be so positive. But with them you can share your worst fears, even your anger and frustrations, and you know they'll understand."

"Sure there are lots of problems. But you can't dwell on them. We celebrate every victory. Every time Christine learns a new skill or crosses a hurdle we throw a party. She probably doesn't realize what they're for, but it helps us!"

"It really helps to see other families and see that they got through. You see that they have all the same problems—or even worse ones—and they're still laughing and smiling and taking vacations. It gets you 'up' again."

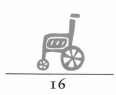

A Suggestion

Look back at the storms you've weathered since your child was born. Congratulate yourself on your strength and resilience.

What helped you get through? Was there something in particular that can help you through future crises?

Isolation

Robert Wade

feel like I'm walking between two worlds."

"You get so caught up in the daily concerns—going to the doctor, going to the therapist, feeding the baby—that's an hour and a half right there. Everything takes so long; you get so exhausted. You spend all day alone dealing with these problems. It starts to feel like that's all there is in life. You feel like no one else has any of these problems. You feel so isolated."

"What are my main concerns? I worry about Michael having to go back into the hospital for another heart surgery. I worry about whether the drugs he's taking are causing side effects. I worry about whether he's going to be terrified by the lab technician next week when he goes in for x-rays and they won't let me stay in the room with him. I worry about how he's going to feel in preschool next year when younger children can do things he can't. These are very pressing concerns for me and I just don't share them with my friends who have normal children. They worry when their kids fall off their bikes and don't get A's in school. I don't have much in common with them anymore."

"I feel like I walk between two worlds. The handicapped world was one I didn't even know existed, and now here I am in it. It separates me from my friends with normal kids. I see less and less of them. I've started to spend time with two other mothers of kids with Down syndrome. That helps because they've gone through what I'm going through and they understand how I feel. And they offer good advice. We make each other go out. I'll say, 'Come on, we'll take the kids and we're going to the movies.' And we do. It helps us not feel so isolated."

"I know that Jason needs to get out and do things—go to the zoo, go to the park, see other children. I try to take him out as much as I can. But it's such a hassle. Getting in and out of the car. Getting the wheelchair in and out of the car. Making sure the other kids have what they need, plus diapers for the baby. Getting everyone

*organized to go. And then you get there and you find
out the place isn't accessible. Or people stare at the
wheelchair and the other kids get uncomfortable…
I know it's wrong—but it's a lot easier to just stay home."*

*"It's been two months since Susan's surgery and I haven't
left the house once except to go grocery shopping. My
husband is starting to go crazy. I really need someone to
talk to. He's the only person I see, and he doesn't know
what to do either."*

Isolation is a very real problem—especially for new parents. During the long days of "nothingness," the inability to seek a way out is equally real. But parents must overcome it because isolation can become damaging—demoralizing them and denying their child vital social interactions. How *do* parents overcome it?

*"I talk to other parents. There's no substitute for that.
You find out you're not alone. You're not the only one
with those concerns."*

*"We went to a parents conference. My husband didn't
want to go. I had to force him. But afterward he really
appreciated it. We both did. We met a lot of other parents
and found out they all have the same problems we have.
It helped us feel normal again."*

Joining a parents group is highly recommended. Special education schools will be able to tell you about ones that exist in your community or about other individual parents whom you can meet. The resource list in the back of this book includes numbers you can call to locate groups in your area.

Other parents find different solutions. For Kathy Taylor, the problem was eased by going back to work.

Going back wasn't her choice. When Bonnie, her daughter with Down syndrome, was six months old, economics dictated that decision.

*"Going back to work was hard at first because I didn't
want to be there. I was emotionally tied to home. But it
was good for me. It got me out, and got me focused on
other things besides Bonnie's problems and my sadness."*

For Cathy Packer, whose first child was born with Down syndrome, help came in the form of having other children. "When all I had was Christian, he was my whole world. I was caught up in his problems and his needs. That was all there was and I felt pretty isolated. But now that I have the other two boys, I'm just as caught up in the 'real world.' It helped me put things in perspective. Plus I have more in common with other parents."

Barbara Collins, mother of eight-month-old Peter who has Down syndrome, joined an infant stimulation program at a Community Board Center. There Peter gets the therapy he needs, and Barbara has a group of parents she can turn to for support.

"Isolation is a choice," says Jo Lynn Lei. "You must not leave a stone unturned in finding ways that will permit you to get out and get help. Just ask! Until David was three I didn't have a regular sitter for him. But then I decided to go back to work and I needed someone who could watch him every day. There was a woman in our neighborhood who had been a school teacher and now was home with her own child. I didn't know if she'd want to watch David or not, but I thought I'd ask. She said, 'Yes.' So you never know until you try. The situation is only impossible if you see it that way."

For some parents isolation is imposed by friends who have a hard time adjusting to the child. The solution? Educate them. "I talk to all my friends about Kevin," says Paula Hightower. "I explain his problems and what we're doing in therapy so they don't have to wonder and feel like they shouldn't ask. I talk about things he can do well, and I bring him when we go out so they see he's just a boy like other boys. The friends who are good friends handle it just fine. The ones who can't handle it, I figure I don't need."

Melissa Surguine-Smith is the mother of premature twins, one of whom has cerebral palsy. She started a support group for parents of premature and high-risk infants to help them get over the sense of isolation they feel from the "real world." The group finds places that cater to children with special needs, and gets their kids out to enjoy the world. "The most important

"The most important thing to remember is that these kids are more normal than they are abnormal. Your child (no matter what kind of handicap he has) is more *like* other children than unlike them."

thing to remember," she says, "is that these kids are more normal than they are abnormal. Your child (no matter what kind of handicap he has) is more *like* other children than unlike them. He likes ice cream, too. He likes hugs and attention, and going to the zoo. Instead of looking at all the ways you *can't* operate in the world, look at all the ways you *can.*"

A SUGGESTION

Find two new people to baby-sit your child. Write their names and phone numbers here:

1. _____

2. _____

Marital Stress

Peter Hoey

"A handicapped child doesn't make a marriage fall apart. Not dealing with your feelings does."

The Collinses: Dave has so many feelings and they're all scary to deal with. He's angry at the situation and angry at the kid and feels guilty for feeling that way. He's angry at his wife for causing it (bad genes!) and feels guilty about that, too. He's terrified of the change, terrified of the economic pressure, terrified that his family is falling apart. He grieves that John won't be the way they wanted him to be, but loves him so much it hurts to look at him. How to deal with that? How to be a father to this foreign child? Confused, he doesn't know what to do; he needs help. And he's angry at his wife for not helping him.

He sees his wife talking to friends and resents the fact that she can do that when he can't. Resents the fact that she gets the sympathy, support and attention as though it weren't his kid, his problem, too. He can't talk to his wife: talking would give reality to his feelings and they're too ugly to express. Besides, he's too angry to talk, and he doesn't want to hurt her. So hating his feelings, he goes off to work where he can be normal.

The Smiths: Harold and Jean go to a meeting at school. It's his first. As they face the team of teachers and therapists, they are told their daughter will never read or write. Jean sits quietly as tears roll down her cheeks. Harold stands up in a rage and cries, "Jean, how can you do this to me?! You'll never get me to come to one of these again!" All this time he'd been going to work, coming home, playing with his daughter, nourishing a dream. Jean had been going to doctors' appointments, therapy sessions, school meetings: she had shielded her husband from the facts. Not on purpose. But she didn't want to hurt him.

In each family, the husband and wife—no matter how similar they may be in other ways, no matter how much in love—have reacted differently to the birth of their child. Each has adopted his own coping style and is angry at the other for coping differently. Each is absorbed in his own needs and feelings, and is unable to see beyond to the needs and feelings of the other. External pressures—differences of opinion on important decisions, economic pressures, reactions of friends and relatives, the needs of other children, sheer exhaustion—all exacerbate the grinding tension. The partners, formerly so close, so familiar, so interdependent, face stormy, frightening isolation.

What makes the situation worse is that it is so hard to talk about. Both parents, caught in their own web of feelings, feel too much pain, blame, anger and guilt to shape easily into words. Both are too afraid of hurting the other to open that emotional dam. Even timing seems to militate against talking, as parents find themselves on an emotional seesaw. When one is "up"—coping, optimistic, ready to talk—the other is down in the depths of depression. This may help the family cope on a day-to-day basis as each parent takes a turn leading the charge, but it doesn't make sharing their feelings easier.

How have parents survived this marital trauma? The first thing they've done is force themselves to look inside, to examine even the most painful feelings, and to share them. By doing so, each has been able to see the other as the person he is, the person he chose to marry, instead of as a symbol of his own frustration.

A second thing they've done, a direct result of the first, is to re-examine the unwritten rules and roles that guide their marriage. George Harris: "I was brought up to believe that the man goes to work and earns money and the wife stays home and raises the kids. But Sharon wasn't going to let me do that." Sharon, his wife, breaks in, "I was doing four therapies a day, 30 minutes each, plus washing, cooking, cleaning and taking care of two kids. I was going crazy. Finally I said to my husband, 'Look, I can't do all this myself. It's not fair for you to go to work, come home and lay on the couch while I cook dinner, do therapy, give the kids baths and put them in pajamas. You have to help.'" George did, but it was hard for him. It shook all the patterns he'd spent a lifetime learning. "You know, it's easier for the wife," he says. "She *expects* to do those activities, so she plans them into her day, but the husband doesn't. Now I do,

> "I was doing four therapies a day, 30 minutes each, plus washing, cooking, cleaning and taking care of two other kids. I was going crazy. Finally I said to my husband, 'Look, I can't do all this myself. You have to help.'"

and that makes it easier."

A third thing successful marriage partners have done is to schedule times when they can be alone together as husband and wife, not as father and mother. "It's not easy," says Bill Sobel, "you don't always get as much time as you need. But it really helps us keep going." He adds, "There are always a hundred reasons why you can't go out tonight, but you've got to do it. I don't think we'd still be married if we didn't."

Lois and Will Lanier have a "date" every Monday night. Nothing is permitted to get in the way. "Usually we go out to dinner or to the movies. Sometimes we're both tired and don't feel like going out, but we go anyway: we'll feel it later in the week if we don't. It's just a time for the two of us to get away from the kids and be together."

Betty Conroy and her husband, Jay, have worked out a reciprocal arrangement with another couple. When either couple needs to get away, their friends will take their children for the weekend. This gives both couples a way to get time alone.

In some ways women are more fortunate in dealing with a child with a disability. Not only are they encouraged by society to express their emotions, they are also, by virtue of their traditional role as primary caretaker, forced to recognize the reality of their child's handicap. Visits to doctors, therapists and schools provide a continual flow of information and assessments. This allows them few delusions about their child's condition. Fathers, on the other hand, are not encouraged to express emotions. Traditionally bound by jobs, they don't often make it to medical and school appointments and don't spend as much time with the child. As a result, they may pretend for a long time that the situation is less severe than it really is. When the truth hits, it hurts all the more for the length of the deception.

So for fathers, coping with a child with a disability can be even harder than it is for mothers. The first thing they need to do is to allow themselves to feel. "I wasn't brought up to have feelings," says Dave Collins. "My father never showed his feelings. He was always strong! I thought I had to be strong too, especially in

> "I wasn't brought up to have feelings. My father never showed his feelings. He was always strong! I thought I had to be strong too, especially in front of my wife."

> "I hated it when he bottled it up inside. I knew he was miserable but he didn't want me to see. That just made me feel like I had to hide my own feelings."

"The family will never be the same. The important thing is to accept that. If you fight change and try to keep things the way they were, you'll only have trouble. If you can be open with yourself and each other, and be open to change, you'll do O.K."

front of my wife. I felt like I had to protect her. But one day I just couldn't hold it in any longer. I went into the bathroom and started to cry. I guess Kathy heard me because she came in. I don't think she had ever seen me cry before. But she put her arms around me and held me... She said afterwards she'd been waiting for me to do that!"

Don Smith was amazed when he went to a fathers group for the first time. "One of the men started crying right in front of everyone. He was a new father and they'd just found out their daughter was blind. He'd just realized that she'd never be able to drive. That broke him up. I thought about that for the next few days. I think it brought me closer to my own feelings."

George Harris feels "richer" for having learned about feelings. "It's like before I was half a person and now I'm whole," he says. He refers to it as "the switch," a turning point in his life. And despite most husbands' fear that breaking down in front of their wives will add to their pain, most wives disagree. "I hated it when he bottled it up inside. I knew he was miserable but he didn't want me to see. That just made me feel like I had to hide my own feelings."

As parents become *emotional* partners, they must also become *informational* ones. Even if fathers can't attend all meetings, they need to hear the information that is exchanged. To shield them is to make their own adjustment harder.

Marital stress is so normal and universal in families with a handicapped child that you shouldn't feel defeated or even surprised at experiencing it. Nor should you feel that you have to handle it by yourselves. The best thing you can do may be to seek help from a marriage counselor. A counselor is frequently able to help parents come to terms with their feelings and help them achieve the open communication they need to be emotional *partners* instead of antagonists. So don't be embarrassed to ask for help. It's a sign of strength to do so.

SUGGESTIONS

1. *For each of you to do…*
   - *Write your spouse a letter. Describe the things he or she does that bother you.*
   - *Set a date when you can be alone for several hours.*

2. Today…*make a date with your spouse. Call the baby-sitter. Put it on the calendar. Don't let anything get in the way.*

Relatives

Shelley Freshman

**T**hey can make it a whole lot easier…or a whole lot harder."

"Through the whole first year my mom was great. She came over and got me out of the house; she made me stop feeling sorry for myself. She baby-sat John so Dave and I could go out together. She was a tower of strength. I don't think I could have gotten through without her."

"When I try to talk to my parents about Christine's problems they say, 'Don't worry; it'll get better. She'll grow out of it.' They're no help."

"At first both of our parents took it pretty hard. I think they felt more pain for us than they did about the baby. But now they're a good support system."

Grandparents have as hard a time accepting a disability as parents do. In some ways, their job is even harder because they feel double grief. They grieve over the grandchild's handicap, but they grieve even more at their own child's pain. Ironically, this second-level grief often leaves them unable to offer the support that their son or daughter needs so much.

In learning to accept the child, grandparents echo the parents' emotions. Just as parents have unspoken fantasies about what their child will be like, grandparents have unspoken dreams for their grandchild. Loss of that hoped-for grandchild causes them grief, anger and anxiety, too. Accepting the reality is even harder for them because they are removed. While parents observe, hold and love their child every day, most grandparents see the child less often. For them, the bonding process that helps parents learn to see the *child* instead of the handicap happens more slowly.

In the process they may make things harder for their children. Betty Conroy: "We called Jay's parents at Christmas, really excited. Paul is four years old and he'd just learned to hold himself up in a sitting position. We said, 'Paul's sitting up now!' And they said, 'Well, when is he going to walk?' They really haven't accepted his disability at all."

Unfortunately, by not accepting the dis-

"'Feed her these vitamins. Give her these tests.' They want me to make her into a different child...They told me I wasn't being a good enough mom."

ability, grandparents can create a tremendous amount of stress and conflict for the parents.

When Kathy and Bob Taylor's daughter, Bonnie, was born with Down syndrome, Bob's large, traditionally oriented family was delighted that they had had a girl. She was the first girl born in that generation. The expectations about how she would behave were numerous and high. When Bonnie failed to meet them, the family was unaccepting. "She'll grow out of it," they said. When she failed to grow out of it, Bob's parents began to put pressure on Kathy. "'Feed her these vitamins. Give her these tests.' They want me to make her into a different child," Kathy sighs. "They told me I wasn't being a good enough mom." Kathy felt justifiably angry and, when the pressure didn't let up, she began to transfer her anger at Bob's mother to Bob. But Bob, too, was feeling the strain. Already torn by his own mixed feelings toward his daughter, he now felt saddled by the feelings of his parents as well. *Their* disappointment and frustration were being transferred to him. Gradually Kathy and Bob became unable to separate their own feelings toward Bonnie from those of the people around them. Communication grew worse, the rift between them grew wider, and the couple was forced into a temporary separation.

Parents can help grandparents accept the disability. The first step is to realize that your parents don't share your intimate perspective. Removed from your child, they may feel the same ignorance and fear that you first felt when he was born. They need to be educated to overcome those feelings.

"My mother had a hard time believing that Susan is handicapped. She doesn't live here so she doesn't see Susan that much. Whenever I'd talk to her on the phone and tell her something the doctor said, she'd say, 'Are you sure? Don't you think you should see another doctor?' Finally, when she was here, I took her to some appointments so she could talk to the doctors herself. Now she's a lot better. I can call her up and discuss decisions with her and she's good at helping me through them. I think she can take a lot more enjoyment out of Susan's small triumphs now, too."

> "It's hard to tell your mother, who has spent your whole life mothering you, that you know more about your kid's condition than she does... Actually, it's not so hard to tell her—it's just hard to get her to listen!"

Despite the fact that most grandparents are eager to learn about the handicap, it's not always easy to teach them. As Becky Licht says, "It's hard to tell your mother, who has spent your whole life mothering you, that you know more about your kid's condition than she does...Actually, it's not so hard to tell her—it's just hard to get her to listen!" To avoid this, it may help to give your parents literature that you've found helpful. This can answer their questions and help them feel informed and involved.

Sometimes grandparents' well-intentioned efforts to help may interfere. "My dad right away set up a trust fund for Bonnie," says Kathy Taylor. "I was glad in some ways—glad to have the financial burden taken care of—but also angry because he didn't set one up for Sam, our older son. I didn't like the fact that he immediately needed to treat her differently."

Educating grandparents is a continual task. As Paula Hightower says, "You need to educate your relatives over and over again, every time you meet new hurdles."

But most parents find the effort worth it. "My father reacted the same way I did," says Craig Packer. "He took it hard at first. It took him a while to adjust. But we talked a lot. He spent a lot of time with Christian. And now his attitude is almost total acceptance. Now he's helpful and understanding."

> "I'm an ambassador for my kids."

Lois Lanier says it best. "I'm an ambassador for my kids. I need to teach other people about handicaps so that they won't be ignorant, fearful and prejudiced. I need to do this with everybody because everybody needs to learn. But I especially need to do it with my friends and relatives because I need them on my side."

A SUGGESTION

Take some family snapshots. Blow them up to 5" x 7". Pick one and write a letter on the back telling your relatives the latest news about your child. Use the other photo and mail them an update once a month.

Siblings

Hunter Freeman

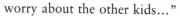

"I don't get much time with my other children because Steven takes up so much time," says Jane Scott resignedly at a mothers group meeting. She, like the other mothers there, recognizes that her non-handicapped children have their own special needs—special because they are themselves unique, and because they are coping with being the sibling of a handicapped child. Each mother worries that she isn't meeting those needs as well as she might. And each wonders how the experience will affect her other children.

Siblings are caught between two worlds: the outside world and the world at home. These worlds place very different demands on them, and they want to do well and be loved in both. Outside the home, a premium is placed on normalcy. All children, through their adolescent years, want to be as much like other children as possible. They want their families to be as much like other families, too.

Within the family, children want almost the opposite. They want to stand out—to feel special in their parents' eyes. Having to compete with a brother or sister who really *is* "special" is difficult. It makes them understandably jealous and resentful.

"Waiting *is what does it to our two other kids,"* says Jane. "*Everything takes so much longer with Steven. They're always* waiting *while we dress him, feed him, load the car. I think that's what they resent the most.*"

For the Buswells it's having Wilson interfere with plans. "In our house you don't ever have a quick dinner and then run to the park. You have a *long* dinner while we feed Wilson, then we drive to the park, and by that time it's getting late and dark and we don't stay so long."

Sadness, anger, guilt, embarrassment: siblings of a handicapped child experience almost all the same feelings their parents do. And like them, they encounter these feelings over and over again each time a new hurdle arises. In the same way that parents sometimes

wish for a non-handicapped child, siblings sometimes wish for a "real" brother or sister, one with whom they could better share their time and feelings. And one who wouldn't make so many problems for them.

Two things make children different from adults in the way they react to a handicap. One is their lack of information. Adults have an informational handle on their child's disability that helps them understand and deal with it. Children don't. They're often too young and inexperienced to understand their sibling's problem. That makes it scary: maybe they'll catch it. Maybe their own children will have the same affliction.

Secondly, children "act out": they behave badly to get attention. Adults have learned to deal with negative feelings in socially acceptable ways. But for children, bad behavior is sometimes the only way they know to get the attention they feel they need.

You can help your children cope in a number of ways. Talking to them when they act out can help them deal with their feelings. "Sometimes when I'm doing therapy or feeding Susan, Tommy will climb on the furniture or pull her hair, just to get attention. I try to be honest with him and say, 'She has special needs and sometimes she needs Mommy more than you do. But you're special too, and I love you both very much.' That little bit of love and attention seems to reassure him. He can usually go back to playing quietly."

Talking about your own feelings helps, too. By modeling good communication skills, you can teach your children to recognize and express their own feelings. Talking isn't always easy, though. Older children may be afraid to tell their parents what they're feeling for fear of hurting them or adding to their burden. Younger children may be unable or unwilling to express emotions.

> "In our house you don't ever have a quick dinner and then run to the park. You have a *long* dinner while we feed Wilson, then we drive to the park, and by that time it's getting late and dark and we don't stay so long."

Claudia Jacobs tells a story about her four-year-old son Gary's attempts to understand why his older sister couldn't talk. Although Claudia had spoken with Gary several times about his sister's handicap, he had seemed uninterested, listening politely but obviously eager to go off and play. One afternoon, Claudia left Gary at a friend's house, where he watched two girls his sister's

35

age playing. Suddenly curious, he asked the girls'
mother why they could talk and his own sister couldn't.
When her friend relayed the story, Claudia at first felt
bad that Gary would talk to her friend but not to her.
After she had spoken with him herself, though, and
found him interested and questioning, she realized that
Gary had not been ready before then to talk. By
discussing it with him earlier, though, she had enabled
Gary to ask his questions when the time was right.

When siblings do talk, the things they say may not be pleasant for parents to hear. Parents want to feel that despite the pressures created by the handicap, their other children are growing up healthy, happy and tolerant. When, instead, they resent the attention the handicapped child receives, or hate the embarrassment he creates for them outside, or wish he were dead (as most do at some time), the goal of family health and harmony seems threatened. We forget that all kids—even those in "normal" families—go through periods of hating each other. As Linda Storrs, mother of six, one of whom is retarded, says, "Give your siblings room to be normal kids!"

"Give your siblings room to be normal kids!"

In fact, studies show that siblings of handicapped children tend to have a *greater* tolerance for human differences, and a *greater* sense of family bonds than other people. Linda describes her son's relationship with his brothers and sisters: "Around the house Steven has to fight like all the rest. They don't give him any special privileges or let him get away with anything. But when they're playing outside, if another kid picks on Steven or makes a wisecrack, they're all over him. No one else can do that to their brother!"

"Matthew is growing up with more compassion than other children because of his sister... although you wouldn't always know it to watch them play together!"

Another mother agrees. "Matthew is growing up with more compassion than other children because of his sister. . .although you wouldn't always know it to watch them play together!"

A second thing you can do to help your children is to look at situations from their point of view. Remember how "normal" you wanted to be when you were that age? Try to minimize their embarrassment. Respect their wishes to not *always* push the wheelchair or baby-sit their brother at outdoor games.

A third thing you can do is balance the "special" things the handicapped child gets with special things for his siblings. "I try to not make it seem like Christian has anything more special than the others," says Cathy Packer. "He's gone to school since he was a baby. So now we're sending Charlie (the next oldest) to classes at the rec center so he can go to 'school' and come home with papers, too."

Giving each of the children special time alone with Mom and Dad helps defuse the jealousy, too. At the Constantines', "Every Saturday morning is Bennett and Lee's time together." In that way, they reassure their non-handicapped child that his place in his father's heart is just as important as his brother's.

Giving the other children specific tasks to do to help their handicapped sibling can also defuse resentment over his extra attention.

"In our house everybody has a task in relation to David," says Jo Lynn Lei. "Julie (age 11) makes his lunch every morning. Mark (12) helps him get dressed. We try to keep their jobs short so they don't resent the time they have to help him. The trick is to enable the siblings to feel involved and useful without feeling so responsible that they become mini-parents."

Involving other children in his routines helps the handicapped child too, making him feel like an integral member of the family. He needs to feel that his role is secure and equal to everyone else's. This means being treated the same way, being taken on the same outings and following the same rules as all the other family members.

"I punish Josh the same way I punish the other kids. Some people think, 'How can you punish a blind child?' But he's got to live in the world just like the rest of them. So he's got to learn the rules."

"We try to treat Susan the same way we treat Tommy. Obviously in some things we can't. But we want her to lead a life that's as much like other children's as possible, and that won't happen if we give her special treatment. It helps Tommy, too, because it reinforces the

rules for him and makes it easier for him to know how to treat her."

In every family, the handicapped child fills a special place. What that place is, and how other children feel about it, is determined to a great extent by the parents. Ellen Powell says it well: "We want our other kids to see Jamie as just another—very important—kid in our family. She's not a handicapped child: she's a child with a handicap. That's a big difference."

"She's not a handicapped child: she's a child with a handicap. That's a big difference."

A SUGGESTION

Today...*make a date with each of your other children to do something special. Just the two of you.*

Peter Hoey

"I t's a tough balancing act."

A group of mothers was talking about how hard it is to balance the needs of a handicapped child against those of the rest of the family. Jan Walters told them this story.

Jan's son, Peter, has cerebral palsy. At the time of the story he was six and had been walking for about a year with the use of braces. Since he was quickly outgrowing his current braces, his therapist was pressuring Jan to buy a new pair. Jan had just gone back to work part-time as a school librarian, in part to help pay for Peter's medical and therapeutic needs. So she and her husband, John, began setting aside a portion of her salary to buy the braces.

That same fall, Peter's sister, Susan, had started kindergarten. Susan had not gone to preschool and was finding the adjustment to school rough. She came home each day in tears, and every morning cried and cajoled, pleading to stay home.

Jan was distraught. She had waited for Susan to begin kindergarten before going back to work, but her daughter's unhappiness made it difficult to concentrate on the new job, and made her doubt the wisdom of her decision. Shouldn't she be at home so she could spend more time with Susan and help her adjust? But she couldn't stay home because they needed her salary to pay for Peter's braces. She was caught in an emotional bind and, silently and guiltily, resented each member of her family for putting her in it. Soon she was snapping at everyone.

John was distressed to find his generally amiable family so unhappy. He was impatient with Susan for her slow adjustment. Her daily tantrums produced irritation rather than sympathy. He didn't understand Jan's sudden temper and coldness. Was she angry that she had to work? Or that the money she earned was going for Peter's braces? Well what about him? He'd had to work and support them all for all these years! He became angry at Jan for taking him for granted and at the same time felt guilty that he wasn't able to meet all of their financial needs himself. Soon he, too, was snapping at the family.

The relative harmony to which they were accustomed had dissolved amidst slammed doors, uncomfortable silences and tears.

One evening after a particularly hard day at work, John came home and poured himself a drink. As he walked into the living room he tripped over a toy that one of the children had left on the floor. The glass dropped from his hand, sending shards and liquid across the room. Even before Jan could come from the kitchen to see what was wrong, John had cursed loudly and stormed out the door, slamming it behind him.

Before he returned four hours later, dinner had been burned, two new toys had been broken and the children had gone to bed in tears. Jan sat on the couch, paralyzed by emotional exhaustion.

John returned at 11:00 p.m., quiet and contrite. He apologized for storming out and in slow, halting sentences, told Jan how difficult the last weeks had been for him. Jan then described her feelings about Susan and the job, and her guilty resentment of the family. As they gave voice to their feelings, both felt the tension start to lift. It had been a trying time for the whole family. Temporary removal from the pressures, they felt, would go a long way toward restoring family unity. So gradually their talk turned to taking a vacation—that one they'd always wanted to take. The timing was right: Christmas was coming up. They hadn't saved for a trip, though...For a moment they looked at each other, each knowing what the other was thinking but afraid to say.

The next day they took the money they had saved for Peter's braces and bought tickets for a trip to Disneyland.

Three years later, Jan still feels they were right to use the money as they did. Peter got his braces—a few months later. But family harmony was restored right away when it was needed most. ◆

A SUGGESTION

Hold a family meeting to talk about how things are...and how they can be better. Set some goals for meeting each person's needs. Meet again in a month to see how you're doing.

〰〰〰〰〰〰〰〰〰〰〰〰

Strangers

Robert Wade

"**S**ometimes you just don't feel like explaining to a total stranger in an elevator."

"I was in the hairdresser's with Jesse and I could hear someone whisper, 'What's wrong with his hands?' I thought I should explain that he has Down syndrome, but I get so sick of explaining...I really just wanted to get my hair cut."

Sound familiar? How often have you bit your tongue when someone asked a stupid question, didn't listen to the answer or demonstrated their abysmal ignorance in a way that really hurt? How many times have you blinked back the tears? Going out in public isn't easy, especially at first.

"At first I felt stares that probably weren't there. It used to bother me a lot. I wanted to stand up and scream, 'Yes, he's a boy! He eats, he walks, he sleeps, just like your son!' But now it doesn't bother me...Well, occasionally it gets me down..."

"In the early days, when my mom came to get me out of the house, we'd go shopping and take Bonnie. When she was a baby, she looked normal. People would stop and say, 'Oh, what a pretty baby!' But I was so angry about the whole thing that instead of saying, 'Thank you,' I'd blurt out, 'She has Down syndrome!'"

Many parents feel in a bind when faced with talking to strangers. On the one hand they hate the stares, hate the stupid questions, just want to buy their groceries anonymously the way people with non-handicapped children do. On the other hand, they know they are "ambassadors" for their kids: by sharing their experiences, they can help shape people's attitudes toward people with disabilities. Kathy Taylor describes a situation in which her own awareness was changed.

"Not long after Bonnie was born I saw a family in a restaurant with a daughter who I thought might have Down syndrome. I was searching for information then so I went up to them and asked the parents if their daughter had Down syndrome. Before they could answer, the girl stuck out her hand and said, 'Yes, my

name is Grace and I have Down syndrome.' I was mortified. But it taught me a lesson about seeing people with handicaps as people."

Jo Lynn Lei describes a situation in which she had a chance to instruct both a stranger and her own son. "I was in a store one day with David. He was in his wheelchair and a woman asked me if he could walk. I said, 'Why don't you ask *him?'* It was a good opportunity for her to see David as a person and for David to practice a response he'll need to give a lot in the future."

In your need to protect yourself and your child, it's easy to be provoked by strangers' stares and questions. It may be helpful to remember that those people don't mean harm: they're just inexperienced and curious. Lois Lanier: "People are ignorant, not mean. They're afraid. It makes them realize it can happen to them. When I realized that, it became easier for me to respond. I realized that I could help them learn about handicaps and that would be better for all of us in the long run."

The opportunities to teach are more numerous than most parents would care for, but sometimes they provide a direct gain.

"When Bonnie was six months old I took her to a baby-sitting co-op. The mother in charge said, 'We don't watch children like that here.' I got hurt and angry, tears welled up and I stormed out. When I got home I thought about it, and I realized that the woman was ignorant. She'd never had any experience with handicapped kids. So I called her back and explained to her about Down syndrome. It's not contagious; here's what Bonnie can do and here's what she can't do. And the woman agreed to let her into the co-op."

As Bonnie has grown older, Kathy's found more reasons to "share her" with the rest of the world. "I'm proud of Bonnie. I'm proud for all disabled kids. Every time she or another child does something great, I want the whole world to know about it. There needs to be more public attention focused on their accomplishments instead of their problems." ·

"I'm proud of Bonnie. I'm proud for all disabled kids."

But even the best opportunities for "public relations" have to take a back seat to your own needs. Sometimes you just don't want to talk. As Lois said, "My response depends on my mood that day. I like talking to people when they're genuinely interested. But sometimes you just don't feel like explaining to a total stranger in an elevator."

Fortunately, improved public awareness can occur as much through your presence as through your words. Jo Lynn Lei tells a story about grocery shopping with her son.

"David and I were in the supermarket when I saw a woman I had known peripherally several years before, before David was born. We nodded at each other in recognition. But then we kept spotting each other as we worked our way across the store. David was having a great time, wheeling up and down the aisles, helping me pick things out. When we got to the other end of the store, the other woman was there, too. She came up to me and said, 'He's having a ball!' I just nodded 'yes.' It was a small thing, but I felt we had helped reshape her awareness a little that day."

Sometimes your non-disabled children can be the best spokesmen of all. Claudia Jacobs tells this story: Her family was in a restaurant when a stranger passing their table stared at Claudia's daughter, Sally. Gary, who was five at the time, took charge. "That's my sister," he said protectively. "She has cerebral palsy, but we love her anyway."

A Suggestion

Write down a response you can give when you don't feel like explaining, but don't want to be rude. Having a response ready will make the situation easier.

Professionals

"T he power they exert over you is enormous..."

"I need them because they hold the key to my child's future. But I get so angry and frustrated by them because they won't take the time to treat me like an individual."

Not being treated like an individual—not being listened to—is parents' greatest complaint about professionals. For many it starts early—with the doctor who first told them of their child's handicap. "They wait for the husband to leave; then they tell the wife. She's alone, totally overwhelmed. When the husband comes back, she tells him what they told her. He has lots of questions. But she doesn't know the answers so he gets frustrated and angry at her. All they've done is set the couple up for conflict at the time they need each other the most. And the doctor is nowhere to be found."

For parents who sense that something is wrong before it's been confirmed by a specialist, getting a doctor to listen is often difficult and frustrating. "I knew when Steven was six or seven months old that he wasn't doing the same things his brothers had done when they were that age. I asked my doctor about it. He just said, 'Don't worry, all babies develop differently.' Every time we went in for a well-baby checkup I'd say, 'He's not doing this yet,' or 'He's not real interested in anything.' The doctor would treat it as if it were *my* problem, as if I were just being overly nervous. Finally, I had the doctor send us to a specialist who tested Steven and discovered he's retarded. Why wouldn't my pediatrician *listen* to me?"

Few parents find ongoing relationships with doctors that are as satisfying as they'd like. One mother sums up her frustrations this way. "I get so tired of being treated like a 'case' instead of like a human being. All I want out of a relationship with a professional is for him to let me be real. And for him to be real with me. Let me be more than just a 2:00 appointment."

School systems draw similar complaints, with two additions. First, schools sometimes undermine parents' own sense of what's best for their child. By positioning themselves as the "experts," and pitting their

> "I get so tired of being treated like a 'case' instead of like a human being. Let me be more than just a 2:00 appointment."

view against yours, they make you question your own judgment about what your child needs.

"It's constant combat at school," says Kathy Taylor. "They know what's best for Bonnie and I'm not doing everything I can for her. I took her to a swimming lesson one day when she had a cold. The teacher said, 'You can't bring her here with a cold! She'll infect the other children!' So the next time she had a cold I didn't take her, and the teacher said, 'If you don't bring her to swimming regularly she won't get the most out of this program.' It's a no-win situation."

The second complaint is that schools' focus is negative. "They always look at what's wrong instead of what's right. It's so depressing to listen to evaluations of your child: 'He is this far behind...' Why don't they tell you what he *can* do instead of what he *can't?*"

Carol Knibbs, whose 14-year-old daughter is retarded: "They're always trying to 'fix' Marti—as if they can't accept the fact that she's handicapped. They spend all their time working on things she *can't* do without giving her a chance to enjoy the things she *can*. It fosters a bad self-image. Everyone buys into it. Instead of seeing a wonderful little girl who loves to play and make friends and be with people, they see a poor little girl who can't walk. Schools need to work more at building self-esteem."

Relationships with professionals do not have to be this frustrating. Instead of contests, they can be partnerships, in which professionals are your allies in serving your child.

Here are some things you can do to make that happen:

1 **Develop positive communication skills.** It's easy for the relationship to become adversarial. But that's counterproductive. You make it easier for professionals to give you what you need if you communicate with them positively.

a) *Be assertive but not aggressive.* Say what you believe firmly, but not with anger or implied threats. Your goal is to get them to listen—not to make them defensive.

b) *Listen.* It's easy to spout a list of grievances. But if you don't listen to the professionals, you can't expect them to listen to you. Your goal is *open communication.*

c) *Act rational.* Dealing with professionals prompts a lot of emotions. Most professionals understand that. Still, the more rational you can be with them, the more willing they'll be to listen.

2 **Find a doctor you can talk to.** You don't have to stay with a doctor you don't like. "Shop around" until you find one you feel comfortable with. Not all doctors feel comfortable with disabilities. Not all are willing to talk about your feelings. Some give parents a lot of information and encourage participation in decisions, others don't. Decide what kind of relationship you want with your doctor and find one who will work with you that way.

As with any two people, sometimes personalities "click" and sometimes they don't. Find a doctor you can talk to easily. As Jo Lynn Lei says, "Good communication is worth waiting a long time in the waiting room for."

Don't feel shy about interviewing a doctor. You hire him to perform a service for you; you should be happy with the service you get. Kathy Taylor: "As soon as a doctor tells me she's 'typical,' we leave him. I won't stay with a doctor I don't like. I look for ones who treat me and my kids the way I want to be treated. When I interview a doctor I ask, 'Have you ever dealt with a child who has Down syndrome before?' If he says 'yes' and implies that all Down kids are similar, I won't go to him. If he says, 'No, but I'll give it a shot,' that's good. You can tell a lot about a doctor's attitude at an interview."

You won't communicate equally well with all the doctors who serve you. Find one with whom you do feel comfortable and ask if he'll help you work with the others.

Hopefully, he'll also give you some emotional support. But that's not the doctor's primary role. A parents group or counselor can better meet that need. The intense anger parents feel toward professionals is frequently a spillover of other anger, guilt and sadness

> "Good communication is worth waiting a long time in the waiting room for."

at having a child with a disability. Counseling can help you come to terms with those latent feelings.

3 You are your child's expert: tell them what you know. You know your child better than anyone. You know what's normal for him. You see sides of him professionals never see. Your gut instincts about what your child needs are correct. Trust them.

Carol Knibbs: "Time after time I'd go into the doctor or the school and tell them what I thought my daughter needed. They'd tell me I was wrong. At first I'd believe them. Then it would turn out I was right. After years of this I finally caught on—I know more about Marti than they do."

> "Time after time I'd go into the doctor or the school and tell them what I thought my daughter needed. They'd tell me I was wrong. At first I'd believe them. Then it would turn out I was right. After years of this I finally caught on—I know more about Marti than they do."

Because professionals see only a small part of your child, they need to hear about what you see at home. Insist they listen. That's not easy: we're trained to see professionals as authority figures who know everything. But they don't; they're only human. So don't be afraid to assert yourself.

Lois Lanier was told by the school that her six-year-old daughter could not read. Lois knew Carrie could read because she saw her reading product names which she had learned from TV. So she made an appointment to speak with Carrie's teacher. When the teacher refused to believe that Carrie read at home, Lois brought out a stack of flash cards. As she flashed each card, Carrie read it correctly. The teacher said, "She's got them memorized in order." Undaunted, Lois shuffled the cards and flashed them again. Carrie still read them correctly. Lois's advice: "Don't be afraid to tell professionals what you see at home."

4 Be prepared. Maximize your time in the office by doing your homework first:

a) Read about your child's condition. Since library books are frequently outdated, ask your professionals or parents group for a current reading list.

b) Make a list of your questions before you go. It will help you remember what you'd planned to ask.

c) If you have a particular concern about your child's health or behavior, keep a log for a few days before you go. Record the frequency and duration of symptoms, plus anything you've done to treat them. This will help the professional diagnose the situation.

5 **Stick to the topic.** A professional schedules time based on what you tell him you need. If, during an appointment, you bring up an "unscheduled" issue, he may not have time to discuss it, and, as a result, may seem hurried or brusque. You can avoid this by stating all your concerns at the beginning of the appointment. If there are unscheduled items, make an appointment to discuss those at another time. Both appointments will be smoother.

6 **Speak up...nicely.** If you have a problem with what a professional has told you, don't be afraid to say so. If you'd like a second opinion, say, "Might someone else in your field feel differently?" Your doctor won't mind: second opinions are common. If you can't squeeze in another therapy at night, ask if there's a different way to get the practice in. Your therapist will help you find one. Work *with* your professionals to provide the services your child needs.

7 **Say "no" to therapy...occasionally.** "The speech therapist says, 'Do half an hour of therapy after dinner.' The physical therapist says, 'Do 30 minutes of therapy in your spare time.' What spare time?! I have two other kids and a husband! I finally said 'no' to all that therapy. I had to choose between being my child's extension therapist and being his mother. And I chose being his mother."

There are times when even an acceptable amount of therapy becomes too much—when your child needs time just to be a child, or when you need time to be with the rest of the family. It's O.K. to say "no" at those times, for a while. Your instinct will tell you when.

8 **Form a partnership.** Professionals are people, too. They have good days and bad days. They work long hours that are emotionally draining. They've chosen their profession because they care deeply about children, and nurse the same hopes for your child that you do. You each have your own—partial—expertise. Together you form a complete team. Make that teamwork happen. *You* are as much responsible for it as the professionals. If you want them to be "real" with you, be

> "The speech therapist says, 'Do half an hour of therapy after dinner.' The physical therapist says, 'Do 30 minutes of therapy in your spare time.' What spare time?! I have two other kids and a husband! I finally said 'no' to all that therapy. I had to choose between being my child's extension therapist and being his mother. And I chose being his mother."

"I make friends with the people who serve my child."

"real" with them. As one doctor said, "Sometimes a little reverse sympathy is very much appreciated. A simple remark like, 'Gee, it looks like you had a tough night,' goes a long way. It solidifies the emotional bond between us."

Eula Boelke says it simply: "I make friends with the people who serve my child." ◆

A SUGGESTION

Be prepared. Make a list of questions now *to take to your next*

- *staffing*
- *doctor's appointment*
- *therapy session*
- *meeting with a teacher*

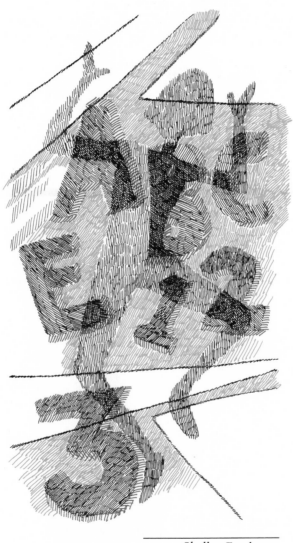

Shelley Freshman

"hinking of myself as Wilson's 'case manager' makes it easier to ask for the things he needs."

Much of the responsibility for your child's education falls on you. It's up to you to coordinate and monitor the many elements that have to work together for your child to get the services he needs. It's a time-consuming task, and some parents find it helpful to think of it as their "job." Barb Buswell: "Thinking of myself as Wilson's 'case manager' makes it easier for me to ask for the things he needs. When I think I can't ask for something *else* for Wilson because they'll think, 'She's a pushy mother,' I remember, 'I'm the manager; it's my job to ask.'

"Sometimes I feel overwhelmed. How can I evaluate this program? How do I know this is best? Then I remember that it's a team approach. I'm not in it alone. It's just my job to get the specialists I trust to talk to each other about it. I remind myself that they know programs, and I know Wilson."

As your child's case manager, you are an important member of his school "team." Public Law 94-142 has made that the case. PL 94-142 guarantees a free and appropriate education to all handicapped children. This education must be delivered in the "least restrictive environment" (the most normal environment possible), and must include any related services, such as physical or speech therapy, that the child needs.

Every three years the school district must assess your child's abilities and needs. You may request to be present for a portion of the testing. More importantly, you *must* tell them about how your child behaves at home. The assessment should jive with how *you* see your child. If it doesn't, something may be amiss. Explain your concerns to the professionals. Perhaps a portion of the test should be redone. If, after a second testing, you still don't agree, you may request to have a third-party assessment done at the district's expense.

Through regular meetings called "staffings," you and the professionals develop and monitor

> "Sometimes I feel overwhelmed. How can I evaluate this program? How do I know this is best?"

your child's Individualized Education Plan (IEP). The IEP is a legal contract between you and the school. It should define your child's needs in very specific terms: "John needs to develop his pincer grasp," not "John needs fine motor development." It should outline the specific type of services he needs to meet those needs: "John needs to work on extension three hours a day," not "John needs physical therapy." It should also list who will provide the services.

It should then include specific long- and short-term goals and objectives: "By January John will be able to prop himself up on his forearms for 15 seconds. We will work on this 15 minutes a day, three days a week." It should prioritize your child's needs, indicating which are most important and will be worked on first.

It's your responsibility to make sure the IEP is written this way. The district may prefer to begin with what services it has available and fit your child's needs to them. It's up to you to make sure that doesn't happen. You must agree with the IEP. The district cannot force you to accept a plan of which you don't approve. Although they request that you sign it, you have no legal obligation to do so, and even if you do, your approval can be revoked at any time. You always have the right to call for another assessment or another staffing at which you can formulate a new IEP.

"As Wilson's case manager I have to ask for the things he needs. But I have to do it nicely."

The staffing is a chance for you and the specialists to assess your child's progress. The specialists should be those who work with your child regularly. They are usually brought by the school system, but you may bring your own if you choose. Staffings can be highly emotional: facing a table of professionals can be unnerving, and the information discussed may be upsetting. Don't go to a staffing alone! Bring another person with you— not your spouse (although he or she should go too if possible) but a friend or relative who will be able to listen more objectively.

Even if you follow the suggestions in *Professionals*, there may be times when you and the school can't agree on your child's program. PL 94-142 establishes a chain of command for resolving such disagreements:

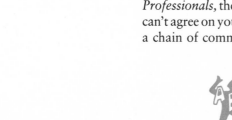

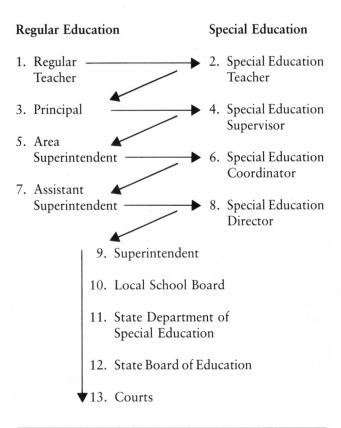

Regular Education   **Special Education**

1. Regular Teacher → 2. Special Education Teacher

3. Principal → 4. Special Education Supervisor

5. Area Superintendent → 6. Special Education Coordinator

7. Assistant Superintendent → 8. Special Education Director

9. Superintendent

10. Local School Board

11. State Department of Special Education

12. State Board of Education

13. Courts

Discuss your concerns with your child's regular and special education teachers. Move up the ladder only as you need to. If you work *with* the professionals instead of against them, most disputes should be resolvable at the lowest levels—among the people who know your child best.

If, by the time you've spoken with the Director of Special Education, you haven't reached agreement, you may request a Due Process Hearing. This is a serious legal procedure, however, in which both sides are represented by attorneys. To request one, contact a lawyer familiar with the rights of the handicapped, but do so only if you are seriously dissatisfied.

That's not to say that you shouldn't fight

for what you believe. But fighting should be a last resort. Diplomacy should be first. As Barb Buswell says, "As Wilson's case manager I have to ask for the things he needs. But I have to do it nicely." ◆

A SUGGESTION

Write down the name of the person you'll take with you to your next staffing.

Is This the Best for My Child?

Hunter Freeman

re we doing everything we can for our child?"

"Is this the best program for my child?" "Is this preschool preparing our child well enough for mainstreaming into kindergarten?" "How do I know if my child's teachers and therapists are well-qualified?"

Such questions are constant. They vibrate restlessly—a background hum in parents' lives.

Rightfully so. Their children deserve the best, and parents should be applauded for wanting to provide it.

For some parents the insatiable need for "the best" masks another desire—the desire to "make up" to the child for bringing him into the world with a handicap. It's like saying, "We feel responsible for causing your problems, so we'll try to make it up to you by giving you the very best services we can find. (Maybe if we *really* give you the best, those services will cure your problems altogether.)"

This search is unrealistic. In most cases parents are not responsible for the handicap and the child cannot be cured. Let go of the guilt. Put your child in the best programs you can find. Then appreciate those programs for being the best. Enjoy your child's progress and renew your self-respect.

Once guilt is out of the way, parents know best what is best for their child. You know your child better than anyone. This doesn't mean you can design his educational and therapeutic program. It does mean that because you live with him every day and can read his moods, you know how well the specialists and their programs are working for him. By having confidence in your ability to recognize when your child is happy, when he is properly challenged and when he is having his emotional needs met, you can have confidence in your ability to give him the best.

Secondly, you alone are best able to provide the most important skill of all—self-esteem. Professionals can create the best program for development of one area. Only you see the whole child and can monitor his challenges and successes to make sure he's happy with himself.

The hardest thing for parents to do is to learn to trust their instincts. Dealing with professionals who are "supposed to know the answers" can easily make you shaky, especially when your opinion doesn't agree with theirs.

"I think I know what's best for my child. At least most of the time I do. But the professionals make you question that. I think the school isn't doing enough cognitive development; they say that social skills are more important now. How do you know?"

The answer: trust your gut. Based on what you know about your child and your own sense of what's important, you know what your child needs. Believe it.

One of the areas in which parents and professionals clash most often is in setting realistic expectations—schools or doctors telling you that yours are too high. Even here, the answer is the same.

Jo Lynn Lei: "You have to trust your gut about what are realistic expectations. Even if the experts tell you it can't happen, if you know or really think it can, you have to give the child every opportunity to try."

Jo Lynn speaks from experience. As described in *New Problems, New Adjustments,* when her son, David, was four, doctors told her he would never walk. They told her to "buy him a chair." Jo Lynn rebelled. "I didn't raise my child to sit in a chair," she declared and didn't buy one. David, who is extremely motivated, became increasingly mobile through crawling but didn't have the strength in his legs to stand by himself. To help him and encourage his mobility, his parents bought him a walker. David enjoyed the walker although his movement in it was difficult. It was more of a prop for standing than an actual walking device. David's new doctors (not the ones who asserted he would never walk) felt that through surgery, David's mobility might be increased. Although it would be a difficult operation and its success was not guaranteed, Jo Lynn felt it worth a try.

To everyone's relief, the surgery was a success. Six months later, when the time came for David's post-op checkup, he insisted on walking with his walker from the car to the doctor's office. After the exam, he walked the thirty yards back to the car. Each trip across the parking lot took 20 minutes. When they reached the car David was visibly exhausted. Jo Lynn helped him into the front seat, put the walker in the trunk and climbed into the driver's seat. David looked over at her and said, "Mom, I did it."

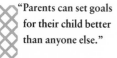

"Parents can set goals for their child better than anyone else," says Jo Lynn. "When I didn't buy him the chair at four, the doctors said, 'That mother, she's unrealistic.' What do you do? You go with your gut."

Kathy Taylor agrees. "I push Bonnie to do the most she can do. She'll let me know if I've gone too far. I look at myself as a competent enough parent to know."

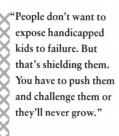

Jo Lynn again: "I *have* to push David for all he is capable of. If I don't live up to my potential, it doesn't matter. If David doesn't live up to his, it will seriously affect the quality of his life."

She adds, "People don't want to expose handicapped kids to failure. But that's shielding them. You have to push them and challenge them or they'll never grow."

Sometimes that means letting a child learn from his mistakes. Sometimes it means letting him try things that you know will be difficult.

"Christian is trying to learn to ride a bicycle because his brothers can," says Cathy Packer. "He has very bad balance and coordination. I really don't think he'll be able to do it. It's painful for me to watch him try. But he needs to do it, so I need to let him."

Your child also needs time to enjoy his successes before moving on to the next challenge. Too often professionals see children's development as stepping-stones, rushing them from one task to the next. Ask them to slow down. Your child deserves every bit of enjoyment and gratification he can milk from each success. A little extra bit of resting on his laurels will do more

Sidebar quotes:

"Parents can set goals for their child better than anyone else."

"People don't want to expose handicapped kids to failure. But that's shielding them. You have to push them and challenge them or they'll never grow."

to bolster self-esteem than it will to delay future gains.

At a conference sponsored by the Special Education Division of the Colorado Department of Education, a group of parents of preschool children sat and listened for two hours as school administrators told them how to be their child's case manager—how to monitor his programs, manage his records, evaluate his progress to make sure he's getting what he needs, and how to demand their rights if they feel he's not. The session was punctuated by frequent questions. Parents were obviously worried that their inexperience would prevent them from getting the best for their children, and that their instincts would prove inadequate. Reading the feelings of the group, Eula Boelke stood up and said, "Here you are, thinking, 'How am I going to manage all this? I just have a little child who happens to have a handicap, and all I want to do is learn to deal with the handicap and love him...' Well, that's *exactly* what you have to do."

SUGGESTIONS

1. *List the instincts you've had about your child that proved correct.*

2. *List the ways you are a good parent to your child.*

Connie Lehman

"W"hat will happen to John after we die? My biggest fear is that he'll end up in an institution."

Thinking about the future can be the most terrifying part of raising a child with a disability. For parents of newborns, it looms as an awesome abyss. Not knowing what their child is capable of, they assume only the worst. Lois Lanier: "When Carrie was born, I could only see her at 30 sitting in a corner. I kept thinking, 'What kind of future will she have?' She was just a baby, but I couldn't stop seeing her in that corner."

As your child gets older and his abilities and potential become more apparent, it's easier to think about the future in concrete terms. But those terms are no less scary. Most people know very little about the options that are open to adults with handicaps, and the options they know about are bleak. As recently as ten years ago almost the only option was life in an institution. Today, people realize that a handicap doesn't have to preclude a normal lifestyle. People with handicaps go to college, have careers, get married and raise families. They live in group homes and hold regular or supervised jobs in the community. They live in residential facilities for the handicapped and work in sheltered workshops. They may be limited by the nature of their handicap—but not by the options society offers.

The most exciting developments are in independent living. An increasing number of programs prepare adults with handicaps to live on their own. Melanie Davis directs one of these programs at Holistic Approaches to Independent Living in Denver. She comments, "We have learned that a person with a disability, regardless of the severity, can live independently with support systems in the community. The important thing," she says, "is for parents to realize this potential for their child, to prepare him for it, and not to limit the child's potential by assuming he can't."

How can you prepare your child for the future?

1 Encourage your child to be indepen-

dent. Don't do things for him that he can do himself. If he can feed himself, let him. If he can dress himself, let him. Try not to give in to the urge to do it for him because "it's hard to watch him struggle" or "it takes too long". If you don't encourage self-reliance now, he'll never be independent later.

2 **Take every opportunity to integrate your child into the non-disabled world.** You want him to live in that world as an adult: you have to prepare him for it now. Make sure the school mainstreams him into regular classes as much as possible. Create opportunities for him to play with neighborhood children. Take him shopping, camping and car-pooling with you. These are not easy things to do. It's hard to put your child into a situation where you know he may get hurt, physically or emotionally. But if he's going to learn to live in the "real" world, he's got to start practicing now.

3 **Make sure your child gets the training he needs in school.** As your child becomes a teen-ager, whether he's college- or vocation-bound, he can take classes in school that will prepare him for that direction. Work with your school to make sure that he gets the classes he needs.

There are also some things you can do for yourself that will help ease your mind about your child's future.

1 **Talk to a lawyer about estate planning and setting up an executorship** so that your child will be able to inherit money. There are legal limits on the amount of money a handicapped child may inherit, and in some cases, an inheritance may jeopardize the child's eligibility for public programs. A lawyer familiar with the rights of the handicapped can help you put together an arrangement that is appropriate for you. (Call the Association for Retarded Citizens to get the name of such a lawyer.)

2 **Find someone who will be willing to take your child(ren) should you die unexpectedly.** No one likes to think about that happening, and hopefully it won't. But the peace of mind you achieve by knowing even that event is covered is tremendous.

3 **Work to effect change.** Changes in

> "Some people are afraid to take their children out in public. I'm trying to teach David to be independent. How will a kid ever learn to grocery shop if you don't take him?"

public attitude and in the legislation that affects the handicapped come about through parents' efforts. Public Law 94-142 was passed because *parents* worked to make it happen. You can help create a better future for your child and others by becoming an advocate for change. Join the Association for Retarded Citizens and other activist groups that lobby for the handicapped. They need parent support. See the resource list at the back of this book for how to contact the ARC nearest you.

Focusing on current problems and working on short-term goals also help many parents turn their anxiety about the future into constructive action. Jan Walters has been working to get her son transferred to a closer school. "I used to be obsessed with the future. I was terrified about what would happen to Peter after we died. But lately, I'm more concerned about today. The future's pretty far away, but Peter has to spend two hours on that school bus tomorrow and the next day. If I can get him transferred I'll feel like I've had a major victory and he'll be a much happier boy. That's bound to help his future!"

> "I used to be obsessed with the future. I was terrified about what would happen to Peter after we died. But lately, I'm more concerned about today."

"The most important thing in planning for your child's future," says Melanie Davis, "is not to plan specifics. Don't plan that he'll live in a group home or that he'll work in a sheltered workshop. That just limits his options. Instead, plan by building his skills now. What skills? Independence, self-esteem, and happiness." ◆

A SUGGESTION

List the things you do for your child that he can do for himself. Decide to let him.

Meeting Your Own Needs

Robert Wade

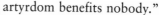

"Martyrdom benefits nobody."

"Just meeting Michael's needs takes all day. When is there *time* to meet my own?" "We'd love to go out to dinner and to the movies like we used to. But Angela's too difficult to leave with someone. No one else would be able to deal with her." "My mother-in-law flew me out for a three-day weekend to give me a breather from the kids. I felt so guilty the whole time I was miserable."

There are a million reasons why you can't find time to meet your own needs. The fact is that finding time for yourself is not a luxury: it is essential. If you haven't met at least some of your needs for relaxation, privacy and emotional support, you won't be very good at meeting the needs of those who depend on you. Martyrdom benefits nobody. And neither does feeling guilty about the time you take for yourself. Guilt only dilutes its benefit to you.

"It took a long time to learn that one. But I finally recognized that at times my own needs come before the rest of the family's. If I don't say, 'I'm taking a day off,' every once in a while, the family reminds me that I'm not a very good mom or wife afterwards."

"I've learned to take time for myself. Now I can do things just for me. I still feel guilty about it, but at least I do it. The first time I did it, I bought a suit. I hid it in the closet for weeks! Finally, I was able to wear it."

"I try to work at patting myself on the back. I know I have to realign my expectations of myself—stop expecting myself to be supermom, superwife, superworker."

"I feel guilty at sending my kid to day care just so I can have time to myself—but it's great!"

It's hard to look at your child's many needs and decide to override them with your own. Obviously, you can't do that all, or even most, of the time. There are times, however, when putting your own needs first will benefit your child more in the long run.

"I work, and I can't always get time off to take Bonnie

*to appointments or to go to meetings at school," says
Kathy Taylor. "I struggled a lot at first with whose
needs came first—hers or mine. I finally decided mine
did, because what she doesn't get today won't ruin her
life, but if I miss my job, I could lose it. Without the job,
there's no money to get Bonnie everything else she needs."*

Parents have found a variety of ways to meet their own needs. Lois Lanier's house is filled with crafts projects. Crocheted afghans, crewel embroidered pictures, watercolors and ceramic sculptures cover bookcases, chair-backs, table tops and walls. The careful, manual labor and creativity that each of these crafts demands, and the rapid progress and finished product she can see with each one, provide Lois relaxation and satisfaction.

Jane Scott looks forward every week to her mothers group. It's her chance to "take off the uniform" she wears the rest of the week and relax, by talking openly with other mothers about problems—and solutions—they all share. Sometimes they don't talk about their kids at all. But the friendship they've developed revitalizes each participant.

Chris Russell was a professional artist before she gave birth to her son. While she had intended to continue as a freelance artist after Michael's birth, the amount of time he demanded made that impossible. As Michael became more mobile, Chris discovered the lack of appropriate therapeutic toys for children with disabilities. She decided to combine her need to do artwork with her knowledge of handicaps and is now building a prototype rocking horse which will safely and enjoyably improve the muscle tone of children with cerebral palsy. The horse has no deadline so Chris can work on it when Michael's schedule permits.

Carol Little has a good friend with whom she has a tacit agreement. Her friend knows Carol well enough to know when she needs to get away. When Joan sees the signs, she offers to care for Carol's son for the day. Carol knows she has to agree. She's allowed to call once during the day to hear that everything is fine.

Every Thursday night Jim and Nancy

Otto drop their two children off with Nancy's mother so they can spend an evening alone together.

In each of these ways, parents find time to meet their own needs. Experience says it can be done!

A SUGGESTION

Plan two things you'll do for yourself *this week. Write them on the calendar now.*

Chronic Sorrow

Allen Birnbach

 hate birthdays."

"I thought we'd handled it real well at first...but things still set me off. What ifs: what if she weren't handicapped—what would she be doing now? How much easier would our lives be? I think back to when Sam was her age—what was he doing, what were we doing then? And I get real angry again."

"David's birthday always makes me melancholy. Apparently, it does that to him, too. On his last birthday he said, 'Mom, I hate C.P.' I said, 'So do I.' He said, 'Yeah, but you don't have it.'"

"My goal is to, one year, get through the whole Christmas program at school without crying."

"I get sad and angry and jealous at other people who don't have to do so much for their kids. Sometimes I just want to lie outside in the sun all day like my neighbors do while their kids play by themselves... but I can't."

"Last week we got caught in a traffic jam of people going to a high school graduation. I got real blue thinking about those kids graduating..."

"One day I went outside and saw my husband sitting in his truck crying. He'd just realized he would never see Bonnie in a prom gown."

The sadness, the pain, the anger don't go away. Even the most accepting, best adjusted, most positive people don't "get over" those feelings as they go on to make the best of their lives. The feelings are always there—under the surface—ready to be retriggered by new events. Birthdays, holidays, milestones (the year she would have learned to drive...), seeing other children his age, all tap into that well of "chronic sorrow."

The feelings don't go away—but they do get easier to deal with. Each time you experience them they are less intense. They are *never* as overwhelming as they were at the beginning.

For some that process begins with let-

"I used to be obsessed with why this had happened to us. Every time I saw another mother with a kid Ben's age I'd get so angry. I'd think, 'What did I do to deserve this?' Once I let go of the 'why' it got a lot easier."

ting go of the "why"—releasing the need to find an answer for why it happened to you and accepting the fact that it did. "I used to be obsessed with why this had happened to us. Every time I saw another mother with a kid Ben's age I'd get so angry. I'd think, 'What did I do to deserve this?' But I think that was just a way of refusing to accept it—as if, as long as I kept fighting it, maybe it would go away. But all it really did was keep me hooked into those terrible feelings—all that pain and anger. Once I let go of the 'why?' it got a lot easier."

The process gets easier because you've been through it before: you know you can survive. And it gets easier because of the new perspective you've gained. What was initially a senseless insult is now a child you love: that makes everything more bearable. Carol Little: "At the beginning I was so angry—at fate, at God, at life, even at Mark—because this had happened to us. It seemed so senseless. The handicap seemed so overwhelming— that was all I saw. But now, compared to who Mark is as a person, the handicap is secondary. I still get sad and angry about it; I wish he didn't have it. But everything about his handicap is so much easier to handle now because it's all part of *him*."

Mark Buswell: "Being the parent of a handicapped child is like walking up a mountain trail. You know how you walk a little way uphill and then the trail makes a U-turn back on itself? After you've turned the corner you can look back on where you've been. That's kind of what it's like to be the parent of a handicapped child. At each new stage of growth you can look back and get some perspective on where you've been. And each time it gets a little easier." ◆

A SUGGESTION

Some people find preparing for a hard time makes it easier to deal with. Think ahead to events that may trigger sadness. Plan activities that can help you get through. Perhaps it's calling an old friend or taking a short vacation. Maybe it's just thinking about events ahead of time so you're ready when they come.

Connie Lehman

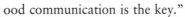

ood communication is the key."

"Put it at the top of the list!" they said. A group of parents was discussing techniques they had used to deal with the pressures of raising a child with a disability. There was no debate about the most important one: good communication.

Good communication has to take place on three levels they felt: between husband and wife, between parents and pros, and between "the head and the heart."

Husband and Wife: Every couple agreed: talking was the glue that kept their marriage intact. It hadn't been easy: all partners had to learn to say things that are more easily left unsaid. All had to force themselves to express the anger, the disappointment and the needs that are hard to put into words. Equally hard was learning to listen and learning to compromise so both partners could have as many as possible of their needs met. But all agreed that their marriages were stronger now for the effort. The new level of communication had spread to all aspects of their relationship—not just their dealings with their children. Most people cherished the new insights they had gained about the person they thought they knew so well.

Parents and Pros: This one, they agreed, was the most difficult. It's hard to "fight nicely in the face of frustration." "The professional shell is a tough one to crack." But all the parents could point to individual instances in which they had talked to a professional quietly and openly about their feelings, and in which the professional had responded in kind. More of these instances are needed. Professionals need to listen more openly to parents. Parents need to give professionals more positive encouragement to do so. They need to form partnerships to work *together* for the benefit of their children.

The Head and the Heart: Well, on second thought, maybe this is the hardest one of all. We live in a society that worships the intellect. Thinking away pain is our nation's aspirin. Unfortunately, it's a short-term solution. Pretending you're happy doesn't banish your pain. Suppressing your feelings only keeps you in their grip. We need to quiet the voice of reason and listen to our feelings. That way we can accept them, learn from them and move on. ◆

A Suggestion

Everybody needs someone to talk to. Your spouse, a friend, a counselor, a theologian…Keeping feelings inside is unhealthy. If you don't have someone now, call one of the agencies listed in the resource section of this book. They'll help you find someone to talk to.

Personal Growth

Lib Cummings

"If you had asked me ten years ago could I do the things I've done in the last ten years, I would have said, 'No way.'"

"Raising John has been the hardest thing I've done in my life. And, you know, I feel better about myself now than I ever have before."

Hard as it is—*because* it's so hard—parents find that raising a handicapped child strengthens them in many ways. It unlocks potential they didn't even know they had.

Kathy Taylor had had no intentions of developing a career before she gave birth to Bonnie. But when Bonnie was six months old, economics required that Kathy work. She reflects on what she's learned over the last three years. "I have capabilities I didn't know I had. I've been able to be a full-time mom *and* hold down a job. I think, 'What if she hadn't been handicapped? Where would I be now?' I probably wouldn't be at this job or this committed to doing both things so well."

Deborah Stein found other strengths: "I've learned that I'm not afraid to take a stand. I just argued with Michele's school about a program they're cutting and I won. I can't believe it! I never thought I'd do that. If it weren't for Michele I wouldn't have."

Linda Chavez concurs. Although she had never been a joiner or an activist, dissatisfaction with programs at her daughter's school prompted her to speak out and work with the school to implement changes. When she met with success she was encouraged to continue. Now she's a "resource mother" for the school district whom they call for advice in structuring new programs. "It's helped me as much as it's helped the kids. It's helped me meet people. I've done things I never thought I could do (like talk in front of City Council!). It's given me opportunities I never would have had otherwise. It's also relieved a lot of the anger and frustration I felt about the system. I feel like I'm helping it be better for someone else."

Lois Lanier also finds inner satisfaction in helping other people. "I remember the first person I talked to who also had a Down child. She came to visit

> "I have capabilities I didn't know I had. I've been able to be a full-time mom *and* hold down a job. I think, 'What if she hadn't been handicapped? Where would I be now?' I probably wouldn't be at this job or this committed to doing both things so well."

me shortly after I brought Carrie home from the hospital. She was so helpful to me—just to see that you didn't die or fall apart because your child has Down syndrome. She still enjoyed life. I wanted to do that for other people so I started visiting other new parents of Down children. I've seen a lot of them. I don't remember most of them, but I'll tell you, they remember you. One day a woman came up to me at school and said, 'I know you.' I said, 'No you don't. I don't know you.' She said, 'Yes, I do. You came to talk to me when I was in the hospital with Timmy. The things you said and the books you gave me to read were so helpful to me then; I've always wanted to thank you.'"

For Melissa Schiff visiting new parents had another benefit. "I started visiting new parents when Beth was six months old. It helped *me* as much as it helped them. I was still pretty new at it, but talking to them made me feel I really had a handle on the situation!"

For Barbara Collins the experience has produced a healthier perspective on life. "This has given me a sense of what's important. I can't empathize anymore with my friend whose day is ruined because the cleaning lady didn't show up!" She adds, "I've also learned to deal with my feelings. I used to hold them in. Now I'm better at feeling and expressing them."

Bill Sobel agrees. "It strengthens you as a parent if you're willing to look at your feelings and work through them. I'm a fuller person now. Before I was only half a man; now I'm whole. I'd choose a different way to learn it next time! But I love my son, and I wouldn't change him now."

For all these parents the best result is greater self-respect. Through the challenges, the hardships and the joys, each one has discovered a new person within. For all of them it is a person they really like.

> "This has given me a sense of what's important. I can't empathize anymore with my friend whose day is ruined because the cleaning lady didn't show up!"

SUGGESTIONS

1. *List two things you can do now that you couldn't do two years ago.*

2. *Name two things about yourself you really like.*

79

THINGS TO CONSIDER

To help yourself and others:
- *join a parents group* to share problems, concerns and solutions and to get support from other families

- *start a parents group* by organizing parents at school

- *visit parents of newborns* to help them adjust

- *work with your school* to create better programs

- *conduct training sessions for pediatricians and hospital nursery personnel* on how to work with parents

- *conduct training sessions for teachers and administrators* on how to work with parents

- *write letters to legislators* requesting funding and legislation for programs for the handicapped

- *join the Association for Retarded Citizens* or other groups that work for change

- *do "public awareness"* when you're out with your child by talking to strangers about handicaps

Advice from Parents

1. *Remember that your child is more* like *other children than unlike them.*

2. *Take time for yourself: don't be a martyr.*

3. *Help is available: don't be afraid to ask.*

4. *Talk to other parents: join a parents group.*

5. *Trust your gut! You are your child's expert; you know what he needs.*

A SUGGESTION

Make a list of all your child's successes. Make it a chart. Put it up in the kitchen where you can add to it every day. Have a celebration for each one.

Allen Birnbach

Don't be alone! Whether you need answers to a medical question, assistance in finding a baby-sitter, or just someone to talk to, there are many agencies to turn to for help. The following is a guide to some of the services available.

Many of these resources have branches on the local level. Check your phone directory for listings of comparable agencies/organizations in your community.

INFORMATION AND REFERRAL SERVICES

Accent on Information
P.O. Box 700
Bloomington, Illinois 61702
(309) 378-2961

Accent on Information is a computerized retrieval system that provides information about products, resources, and the like for disabled persons. (There is a nominal fee for this service.)

American Society for Deaf Children
814 Thayer Avenue
Silver Spring, Maryland 20910
(310) 585-5400 [V] (301) 585-5401 [TDD]

The American Society for Deaf Children provides information and referral about deafness and raising deaf and deaf-blind children to professionals and families of deaf persons. More than 100 affiliated support groups are available for parents nationwide. Information is also exchanged through a resource library, a bimonthly members newsletter, and a biannual national family convention.

Association for Children with Learning Disabilities, Inc.
4156 Library Road
Pittsburgh, Pennsylvania 15234
(412) 341-8077

The Association for Children with Learning Disabilities, Inc. (ACLD) is devoted to the well-being and education of children and adults with learning disabilities and will respond to requests for information on any related topic. The ACLD has more than 800 state and local affiliates throughout the nation. Information on chapter locations as well as a free packet about the ACLD may be obtained on request. A list of materials from the association's resource center is also available free of charge.

Association for Retarded Citizens
National Headquarters
2501 Avenue J
Arlington, Texas 76011
(817) 640-0204

The Association for Retarded Citizens (ARC) is the largest voluntary organization in the United States devoted solely to the welfare of disabled persons and their families. The ARC works on the national, state, and local levels to provide services, guidance, advocacy, free public educational opportunities, and resources to parents and other individuals, organizations, and communities concerned with solving the problems caused by retardation.

Clearinghouse on the Handicapped
(Department of Education)
Switzer Building, Room 3128
400 Maryland Avenue, S.W.
Washington, D.C. 20202
(202) 732-1245

The Clearinghouse on the Handicapped furnishes information about a wide variety of resources available nationwide for physically and/or mentally disabled children and adults.

Council for Exceptional Children
1920 Association Drive
Reston, Virginia 22091
(703) 620-3660

The Council for Exceptional Children (CEC) works to advance the special education needs of children with specific learning disabilities. It also serves children with emotional, cognitive, motor, visual, auditory, or communication handicaps, as well as gifted children. The CEC maintains a collection of special education literature for parents, teachers, and administrators through its Department of Information Services. It also coordinates and supports a network of local chapters and state and provincial federations, and it represents specific areas of interest within the field of special education as well.

Easter Seal Society
National Headquarters
2023 West Ogden Avenue
Chicago, Illinois 60612
(312) 243-8400

The Easter Seal Society serves handicapped children and adults. In addition to information dissemination and referral, its services include public education, counseling, recreation, equipment loan, evaluation, and rehabilitation. The Easter Seal Society also acts as a funding source for therapy and rehabilitation equipment. During the summer months, Easter Seal Handicamps offer resident camping (recreation and rehabilitation) to adults and children who are mentally retarded or have physical disabilities.

Let's Play to Grow
Joseph P. Kennedy, Jr., Foundation
1350 New York Avenue, N.W.
Suite 500
Washington, D.C. 20005
(202) 393-1250

Let's Play to Grow (LPTG) brings the delights of play and shared experiences into the lives of developmentally disabled persons, their families, and friends. It uses an international network of family activity clubs and specially designed play guides. Parents and siblings can use LPTG within the family or through family groups. Resource guides are also available.

March of Dimes
National Headquarters
1275 Mamaroneck Avenue
White Plains, New York 10605
(914) 428-7100

The March of Dimes makes available printed and audiovisual materials dealing with disability awareness. It also offers referrals to (and limited funding for) organized parent support groups.

National Association of Developmental Disabilities Councils
1234 Massachusetts Avenue, N.W.
Suite 203
Washington, D.C. 20005
(202) 347-1234

The purpose of the National Association of Developmental Disabilities Councils is to educate the public and exchange information about the needs and rights of developmentally disabled persons. It assists state and territorial councils in developmental disabilities–related matters affecting states, territories, and the nation.

National Down Syndrome Congress
1800 Dempster Street
Park Ridge, Illinois 60068
1-800-232-6372

One of the primary purposes of the National Down Syndrome Congress (NDSC) is to reach out through its approximately 600 groups to offer parent support to families of children with Down syndrome. It also provides annual seminars for the leadership of these parent groups to keep them up to date in the newest areas of interest. These programs are held concurrently with the yearly two-day convention for parents, professionals, and other interested persons.

National Federation of the Blind
1800 Johnson Street
Baltimore, Maryland 21230
(301) 659-9314

The National Federation of the Blind (NFB) is the largest, oldest, and most active organization of the blind in the country. Its purpose is the complete integration of the blind into society on a basis of equality. The NFB has chapters in every state and major city in the country. *Future Reflections,* a quarterly magazine of the NFB, is published for the parents of blind children.

National Information Center for Handicapped Children and Youth
P.O. Box 1492
Washington, D.C. 20013
(703) 522-0870

Funded by the United States Department of Education, the National Information Center for Handicapped Children and Youth (NICHCY) acts as a clearinghouse for anyone seeking information about children with handicaps. Parents may receive publications and fact sheets about specific disabilities, addresses of parent organizations (local, state, and national), legal information, ideas on how to work with schools and other agencies, and informative newsletters.

National Library Service for the Blind and Physically Handicapped
1291 Taylor Street, N.W.
Washington, D.C. 20542
(202) 287-5100

The collection of the National Library Service for the Blind and Physically Handicapped (NLS) includes full-length braille and talking books and magazines produced for blind and physically handicapped readers. The children's collection includes a number of special books that combine print with braille, enabling blind and sighted children and adults to read together. Collection materials and playback equipment provided by NLS are distributed through a national network of 160 locally funded cooperating libraries and agencies. These items are loaned free to individuals who cannot hold, handle, or read conventional printed materials. An application for the Talking Books Program may be obtained by writing to the National Library Service for the Blind and Physically Handicapped.

Parent Information Center
P.O. Box 1422
Concord, New Hampshire 03301
(603) 224-7005

The Parent Information Center is a nonprofit organization that provides information, support, training, and consultation to parents of children with disabilities. The center also has a variety of materials available to parents and professionals and a number of books that can be ordered.

TASH: The Association for Persons with Severe Handicaps
7010 Roosevelt Way, N.E.
Seattle, Washington 98115
(206) 523-8446

TASH functions to support quality education and independent life-styles for persons who have experienced severely disabling conditions. Requests for information and referral are welcomed, although there are nominal charges for some of these services. Membership includes families, educators, lawyers, medical personnel, and others concerned with issues of human dignity.

United Cerebral Palsy Association, Inc.
66 East 34th Street
New York, New York 10016
(212) 481-6300

The United Cerebral Palsy Association (UCPA) promotes the prevention of cerebral palsy and provides services ranging from information and referral to infant programs for those affected by cerebral palsy and for their families. Parents of children recently diagnosed as having cerebral palsy will be referred to one of the organization's 220 affiliates nearest to them.

United Way of America
701 North Fairfax Street
Alexandria, Virginia 22314-2045
(703) 836-7100

The nation's 2,200 United Ways support a variety of human care services. Included among these services are programs for disabled children and adults.

Through its 400 information and referral services, the United Way offers information about child care, special services, and other resources for children and adults with disabilities.

HEALTH CARE

Muscular Dystrophy Association
810 Seventh Avenue
New York, New York 10019
(212) 586-0808

The Muscular Dystrophy Association (MDA) supports a worldwide research program directed at finding the causes of and treatments for muscular dystrophy and related neuromuscular disorders. Through a nationwide network of 240 MDA clinics, the association provides diagnostic services and rehabilitative follow-up care. Some 175 chapters throughout the country assist with payment for services, which include physical, occupational, and respiratory therapies; orthopedic equipment; respiratory equipment; transportation aid; and flu shots. MDA chapters also sponsor self-help groups for those with neuromuscular disorders and for their families.

Shriners Hospitals for Crippled Children
P.O. Box 25356
Tampa, Florida 33622
1-800-237-5055
In Florida: 1-800-282-9161
In Canada: 1-800-361-7256

Shriners Hospitals for Crippled Children provide medical care, free of charge, to children up to their eighteenth birthday. Among the services available to patients are diagnostic services, inpatient and outpatient care, and surgery. Any child is eligible for admission if, in the opinion of the hospital's chief of staff, the child would benefit from treatment and if treatment at another facility would place financial burden on the family. There are currently 19 Shriners Hospitals operating across the country.

Ronald McDonald House
500 North Michigan Avenue
Chicago, Illinois 60611

Ronald McDonald House offers lodging, for a nominal fee, to families of a seriously ill child during the period of the child's treatment at an out-of-town health care facility. Each house is owned and operated by a locally funded nonprofit organization. There are currently more than 100 houses operating throughout the world.

LEGAL AID

National Association of Protection and Advocacy Systems
1719 Kalorama Road, N.W.
Washington, D.C. 20009

The purpose of the National Association of Protection and Advocacy Systems (NAPAS) is to further the human, civil, and legal rights of persons with disabilities, to advance the interests of member organizations, and to enhance their capacity to provide optimal services. NAPAS is composed of members from the 50 states and 6 territories that have a designated protection and advocacy system for persons with developmental disabilities. Information about the location of member organizations may be obtained by contacting the Legal Center Serving Persons with Disabilities, 455 Sherman Street, Suite 130, Denver, Colorado 80203, (303) 722-0300.

ADVOCACY

Association for Retarded Citizens
Governmental Affairs Office
1522 K Street, N.W.
Suite 516
Washington, D.C. 20005
(202) 785-3388

The Association for Retarded Citizens has among its major goals the establishment and improvement of services and benefits to persons who are mentally retarded. A Governmental Affairs Committee sets yearly legislative goals and monitors the implementation of programs and regulations. A booklet describing the ARC's legislative goals can be obtained from the Governmental Affairs Office.

BOOKS

The following books are suggested reading for parents who are dealing with the emotions of having a child with a disability:

A Child Called Noah and *A Place for Noah,* by J. Greenfeld

The Chronically Ill Child, by Audrey McCollum

A Difference in the Family, by Helen Featherstone

Educating Exceptional Children, by Samuel Kirk and James Gallagher

Helping Your Exceptional Baby: A Practical and Honest Approach to Raising a Mentally Handicapped Child, by C. Cunningham and P. Sloper

Home Care for the Chronically Ill or Disabled Child, by Monica Loose Jones

Hope for the Families, by Robert Perske

Journey, by R. Massie

Like Normal People, by R. Meyers

Mental Retardation in School and Society, by D. L. MacMillan

Parental Attitudes toward Exceptional Children, by Harold Love

Parents Speak Out: Views from the Other Side of the Two-Way Mirror, edited by Ann Turnbull and H. Rutherford

Raising the Handicapped Child, by Laura Perlman and Kathleen Anton Scott

Recipes for Fun, created by Let's Play to Grow of the Joseph P. Kennedy, Jr., Foundation

Special Children, Special Parents, by A. T. Murphy

When Bad Things Happen to Good People, by Harold Kushner

PUBLICATIONS

Accent on Living
P.O. Box 700
Bloomington, Illinois 61702
(309) 378-2961

Accent on Living is a quarterly magazine for the disabled that includes information about medical updates, new products, family relationships, travel, and so on. Also available are Accept Special Publications—unique, affordable books on disability-related topics.

The Exceptional Parent
Subscription information:
605 Commonwealth Avenue
Boston, Massachusetts 02215
(617) 536-8961

Published eight times a year, *The Exceptional Parent* provides timely articles and resources for parents and professionals involved with the education and care of children who have disabilities. This magazine is an outstanding source for ideas, inspiration, and current information.

Getting Help for a Disabled Child— Advice from Parents
Available through
Public Affairs Pamphlets
381 Park Avenue South
New York, New York 10016
(212) 683-4331

Sharing Our Caring
Available through
Caring
P.O. Box 400
Milton, Washington 98354
(206) 922-8194

Sharing Our Caring is a journal written especially for parents of children with Down syndrome. Each issue provides a forum for parents to share their experiences and exchange information and resources. An extensive listing of publications, audiovisual materials, and parent groups is also available. *Sharing Our Caring* is funded through contributions and is published four times a year.

DIRECTORIES

Directory for Exceptional Children
Porter Sargent Publishers, Inc.

This guide lists (by state) the educational and residential facilities available for children with different types of emotional and physical disabilities. Information on each treatment center includes the ages and sex of the children accepted, the cost, the types of therapy available, the number of staff, and a brief description of the facility. The directory can be ordered through the Exceptional Parent Bookstore, 605 Commonwealth Avenue, Boston, Massachusetts 02215.

A Reader's Guide for Parents of Children with Mental, Physical, or Emotional Disabilities
Available through
Exceptional Parent Bookstore
605 Commonwealth Avenue
Boston, Massachusetts 02215

The *Reader's Guide* is a comprehensive resource of books, organizations, and references for parents of children with disabilities. It is divided into six categories: (1) books relevant to all disabilities—includes personal accounts, instruction in the home, and special education; (2) selections of specific disabilities; (3) books under specific topics of interest to parents, professionals, and persons with handicaps; (4) books for children about children with disabilities; (5) listing of references written by persons with disabilities; and (6) listings of journals and directories in addition to indexes of organizations, authors, titles, and publishers.

FILMS

Corporation on Disabilities and Telecommunication (CDT)
P.O. Box 27573
Los Angeles, California 90027
(213) 836-5124

Corporation on Disabilities and Telecommunication (CDT) strives to involve people with disabilities in the media. Its primary goals include providing training and employment opportunities in the field of telecommunication and developing programs that realistically reflect the culture and daily life of disabled individuals.

Every year CDT sponsors "Superfest: A Film Festival on the Exceptional Individual," which offers a forum for presenting and evaluating approximately 150 films concerning the lives of disabled children and adults. Catalogs of the films previewed and those that received awards are available from CDT.

Kids with Canes
Available through
Nebraska Services for the Visually Impaired
4600 Valley Road
Lincoln, Nebraska 68510
(402) 471-2891

Kids with Canes is a videotape depicting children as young as five years of age receiving cane-travel instruction. Parents of the children also describe their feelings and reactions about their child's increasing independence and mobility.

This Child Is Not Alone
Available through
Rocky Mountain Child Development Center
University of Colorado Health Sciences Center
4200 East 9th Avenue
Denver, Colorado 80262
(303) 394-7224

This Child Is Not Alone contains a series of interviews with families who share their experiences of living with a child who has a disability.

What Was I Supposed to Do?
Available through
Arapahoe County Association for
    Retarded Citizens
2200 West Berry Avenue
Littleton, Colorado 80120
(303) 794-9228

This film is a frank and poignant docu-
mentary about parents of children with
developmental disabilities. Personal accounts are interwoven with a physician's
viewpoint, creating a straightforward
and positive approach to families' experiences and emotions.